Pente

and the Catholic Church

Relation and Differences
Future Development

Advantage
BOOKS

Harald G. Huber

Pentecostalism and the Catholic Church: Relation and Differences — Future Development by Harald G. Huber

ISBN: 978-1-59755-394-0

Published by: ADVANTAGE BOOKS™
Longwood, Florida, USA
www.advbookstore.com

Original title: *Pfingstbewegung und Katholische Kirche: Verwandtschaft und Unterschiede – Zukunftsentwicklung* © Copyright 2015 by Schweizer Literaturgesellschaft.

Library of Congress Catalog Number: 2016943169

First Printing: June 2016
16 17 18 19 20 21 22 10 9 8 7 6 5 4 3 2 1
Printed in the United States of America

Introduction

The comparatively rapid growth of Pentecostalism since the beginning of the twentieth century raises the question whether this outpouring of the Holy Spirit might have been predicted in the Bible. Even though the number of official members is still smaller among Pentecostals than Catholics, it is not unreasonable to suppose that Pentecostalism has more practicing members than the Catholic Church.

In my view, there are two main reasons for this. First, Pentecost was the evening before the eighth day of God's working in this world. This was followed by a dark night and then, with the Pentecostal movement, the bright day. The Old Testament prophet Joel, too, predicted this by prophesying about the former and the latter rains, with a time of drought in between.

Second, the Catholic Church emerged in this time of drought. This is predicted in Book of Revelation through the woman in the wilderness who has twelve stars on her head, signaling the twelve Apostles who are conveying the Holy Spirit to her with the goal of endowing the bishops and priests, who received their office in an uninterrupted succession, with the power of the Spirit. However, Revelation also predicts that the woman's conveyance of the Spirit will come to an end at some point, although the times given are only symbolic in character, and it is not clear how the relation between the Catholic Church and Pentecostalism will develop. It is possible that, in future, the Charismatic Renewal will not be the most essential part.

In what follows, I have listed the references I used to support the development I outline in this book. It is my hope that this will contribute to an ecumenical view.

Table of Contents

Chapter 1

The Time until Joachim of Fiore

A. Catholics and Protestant Pentecostals

It is a fact that there are two overarching Christian denominations or groups in the world: On the one hand, there is the Roman Catholic Church together with the Uniate and non-Uniate Orthodox churches, and perhaps also the Anglicans. On the other hand, there are the new Pentecostal groups that, with the exception of few forerunners, only began to emerge in 1901 and experienced a rapid growth after the Second World War. Later, Charismatic modifications of existing denominations contributed to the movement, and, finally, the "Neo-Pentecostals" who cannot necessarily be counted as part of any specific denomination. I rely on the standard reference work, *World Christian Encyclopedia*, 2nd Ed. by David B. Barrett etc.,[1] which, among other sources, uses statistics by the Vatican, as well as on *The New International Dictionary of Pentecostal and Charismatic Movements* by Stanley M. Burgess and Eduard M. Van der Maas.[2]

Based on these works, we can list the following numbers (in millions of people):[3] (See table on next page)

Table 1

It is not clear whether Anglicans should be counted as part of the Catholic/Orthodox group or the Protestant group, which is why the numbers in the table include two variations (Anglicans in brackets, as well as “Others incl. Prot. excl. Angl.“). What is noteworthy are the different Pentecostal renewal movements in the year 2000,[4] accounting for 26.7% of Christians worldwide (534 of 1999), of which 12% are classical Pentecostals (65), 33% Charismatics within traditional denominations (174) and 55% Neo-Pentecostals (295). The greatest percentage of Neo-Pentecostals are in Asia (79%), followed by North America (65%) and Africa (63%). The most significant contributor to this is the growth of Christianity in China where, even after the demise of Mao, it is primarily Neo-Pentecostal house churches that manage to hide from state persecution. In the year 2000, it was estimated that 99% of all renewal movements in China were Neo-Pentecostal, totaling 54 million Christians.[5] By the year 2025, this number is expected to rise to 90 million. Some even estimate a number as high as 150 million,[6] which would be about 10% of the population. In Ancient Rome, the Constantinian shift is said to have happened at roughly 5% percent of the population!

In conclusion, it should be noted that the number of Charismatic Catholics, Orthodox and Anglicans cannot be compared to the number of people in Pentecostal renewal movements, consisting of classical Pentecostals, Charismatic members in traditional denominations and Neo-Pentecostals. In the Catholic Church, many places also count people who are just born and baptized into the Church and pay their taxes or contributions, without necessarily being actual believers or identifying with the, at times, quite spiritual orientation of the leadership of a congregation. (Baptized) children, too, are counted as members. In contrast, Classical Pentecostals and especially the rapidly growing and often persecuted Neo-Pentecostals consist primarily of adults who decided to join a congregation because they truly believe; children are only baptized and counted as part of the congregation when they are adults. In this connection, it is appropriate to mention that persecution and the “blood witness” (that is, the act of martyrdom) make the cross of

Christ real to people, which often leads to unexpected growth, as has been supported by statistics.[7]

B. The Development of the Church before the Present Time

The background of the church situation today goes back to a history that consisted only of Catholics and Orthodox, particularly a 700-year-long epoch in medieval times, which we will still discuss. Today, Catholics and Pentecostals coexist in vast numbers, a fact that must have some kind of theological foundation and be evident in the prophecies of the Bible. There are various points one can make in connection to this:

(a) To start with, one can see the age of the Holy Spirit, which started with Pentecost after the Ascension of Christ, as a new day. According to the Israelite conception, as shown in the Old Testament, a day always begins in the evening. Even today, this is evident in the practices of the Catholic Church where Sunday mass is sometimes held on the night before. In German, another word for Saturday is *Sonnabend*, that is, the evening to Sunday. It is the same with the day of the Holy Spirit. Pentecost and the age of the Apostles are the evening, leading to a dark night before the dawn."[8]

(b) One can refer to the prophecy of Joel: "And do you, O children of Zion, exult and rejoice in the LORD, your God! He has given you the teacher of justice: he has made the rain come down for you, the early and the late rain as before."[8] Joel continues, "Then afterward I will pour out my spirit upon all mankind. Your sons and daughters shall prophesy, your old men shall dream dreams, your young men shall see visions. Even upon the servants and the handmaids, in those days, I will pour out my spirit. And I will work wonders in the heavens and on the earth, blood, fire, and columns of smoke. The sun will be turned to darkness, and the moon to blood. At the coming of the Day of the LORD, the great and terrible day. Then everyone shall be rescued who calls on the name of the LORD."[9] This also seems to be the prophecy to which James referred to in the following verses: "Be patient then, brothers, until the arrival of the Master! Behold, the farmers await the precious fruit of the earth, having long patience for it until (the earth) receives (the) former (rain) and (the) latter (rain)."[10] In this prophecy, "servants" and "handmaids" as well as "farmers" are mentioned, hence not only ordained priests. These are the verses that, starting in 1901, Pentecostals started to use, talking about the "latter rain."[11] Brother Ephraim, a Charismatic who converted to Catholicism, used similar language.[12] Due to the dark age that followed Pentecost, there are still some Protestants today who teach that the age of the Holy Spirit is over. They fail to see that the night is followed by an even brighter day, or, to put it a different way, that the dry season is followed by the latter rain. Their teaching is clearly irreconcilable with developments in recent history.

(c) Another, somewhat more concrete, foundation for the development of the Spirit in the church is the twelfth chapter of Revelation, about a great dragon—that ancient serpent called the Devil, or Satan, who leads the whole world astray. The archangel Michael and his angels fought against this dragon and his fallen angels in heaven and hurled them down to the earth. This means there is no longer any accuser of the "brethren" before God in heaven. But woe to the earth and the sea, because the devil has gone down to them.

Furthermore, there is a "sign in heaven": a woman clothed with the sun, with the moon under her feet and a crown of twelve stars on her head. She was pregnant and cried out in labor pains. She gave birth to a child whom the dragon wanted to devour, but she fled into the wilderness to a place prepared by God for her as a refuge. There, she is being taken care of and is safe from the serpent. "The serpent, however, spewed a torrent of water out of his mouth after the woman to sweep her away with the current. But the earth helped the woman and opened its mouth and swallowed the flood that the dragon spewed out of its mouth."

Pierre Prigent, in his work *Apocalypse 12, Histoire de l'exégèse* ("Revelation 12: An Exegetical History") gives a detailed history of the interpretation of this image. According to him, the first references to this passage come from Hippolytus[14] who lived in the early third century in Rome and was a respected teacher in the church. Unfortunately, not all of his works survive, and we only know them from quotations in other works. This is especially true of his interpretation of Revelation 12. However, his work on the Antichrist does include a partial interpretation of Revelation 12. Then there is an Arabic commentary on Revelation, which often quotes Hippolytus, including his *Apocalypse 12*. In addition, a Coptic text has survived that retains his interpretation of the first six verses of Revelation 12. These seem to be the only reasonably reliable documents at our disposal.

Hippolytus about verse 1: "The woman is the church, clothed with the Logos (the Word of God), adorned with the glory of heaven,[15] for the moon is under her feet. The crown of the twelve stars equals the twelve Apostles through which the church is founded."

About verse 2: "The pain and the cries: the church continuously gives birth to the Word, even in the midst of persecution."

About verse 5: "The son is Christ, God and man, to whom the church continuously gives birth by teaching the heathens. He is raised up, for he is a heavenly and not an earthly king."

The Arabian commentary also interprets the woman as the church with Christ as the sun, but it is more specific in saying that the moon is John the Baptist. The twelve Apostles of the crown are on the head, signifying that they are the beginning of the church.

The Coptic fragment says about verse 1: "The woman is the church of the saints at the time of the Antichrist. The sun—Christ, sun of righteousness, new covenant. The moon is the old covenant." About verse 2: "The pregnancy and the pains symbolize the Holy Spirit [...] whom the saints have received. They are the pains of the fear of the Lord. ... Apparently, what this means is the church of the saints."

There were a number of authors who interpreted Revelation 12 not as a historical prediction but as a purely spiritual picture. This includes Methodius, who died in 312 as a martyr. He, too, believes that the child born of the woman cannot be Jesus of Nazareth, since he thinks that Revelation does not refer to events in the past.[16] By saying this, he might have also rejected the interpretation that the woman is Mary. In his view, the child is Christ in the spiritual sense in which he is born in each believer. It is the image into which every Christian must be formed, even if it requires great pain. At the same time, the child is a picture of the believers. When the Devil attacks them, they are being taken up to the throne of God; their spirits rises up to the kingdom of heaven. Tychonius views the moon under the feet of the woman (the church) as the church of the heretics.[17] Other spiritual interpreters see the woman in

Revelation 12 both as the church and as the virgin Mary, who is supposed to be a picture or archetype of the church.[18]

One interesting interpretation is that of Ambriosius Autpert (written in 758-67).[19] According to him, the battle described in the chapter started with the birth of Christianity and continues on. However, at the end of time, it will reach a more intense climax. And about verse 12: The earth and the sea symbolize the heart of sinners and, more specifically, the Antichrist at the end of time.[20]

Finally, the interpretation of the Jesuits is worth mentioning,[21] beginning with Francisco Ribera who interprets the woman as the church in the last days. He does not identify the woman with the mother of Christ.

I would also like to refer to the work of Wilhelm Kamlah, *Apokalypse und Geschichtstheologie* ("Apocalypse and Theology of History"), which Prigent repeatedly quotes. In an appendix entitled "*Mulier amicta sole* – The Tradition of Interpreting Revelation 12," he portrays Kamlah's work as follows:

"The *Mariological* interpretation of Ap. 12, widely known today, only rarely appears in the commentaries of the early MA. The generally accepted view was: the woman is the church, she has the moon (the world) under her feet, is clothed by the sun (Christ) and carries the crown with the twelve stars (the twelve Apostles). The equation of woman = ecclesia can already be found in Hippolytus. The woman gives birth: the ecclesia is the mother of the believers; through baptism, she gives birth to sons for God. Now, it has always suggested itself that the birth of the child is the birth of Christ. But how can the church be the mother of Christ? This difficulty gave rise to a host of attempted solutions and peculiar equations. To start with, one could go the route of Bruno of Segni by saying: the church gives birth to Christ in the hearts of the believers. One could also say: the believers are the body of Christ, and in this sense the church gives birth to Christ through the believers. And since the church itself is the body of Christ, this can even be brought to the point: '*Ecclesia quotidie gignit Ecclesiam.*' None of these suggested solutions speak of the physical birth of Christ; the spiritual interpretation was valued more highly," etc.

Hugo Rahner, too, in his work *Symbole der Kirche* ("Symbols of the Church"), begins the chapter entitled "The Birth of God / The Teaching of the Church Fathers on the Birth of Christ from the Hearts of the Church and the Believers"[24] by briefly outlining this teaching: "The teaching of Christ being born from the church and the hearts of the believers takes the starting point of the gracious union in Christ not so much in individuals thus graced and their membership in the body of Christ but in Christ himself who is the same in everyone and joins all in the unity of his body, which is the church. Accordingly, we will see how Methodius of Philippi said in his interpretation of the apocalyptic woman: 'The one who gives birth to the male Logos in the hearts of believers is the our mother, the church.' This theology of the birth of Christ by the church culminates in the almost dialectical statement that the church, because it gives birth to the body of the mystical Christ, actually gives birth to itself!"

To elucidate this point: The twelve stars, symbolizing the twelve Apostles, show that the Holy Spirit now comes through these Apostles and no longer through his free blowing on and through the sea, which is being polluted by the evil spirit of the Devil. The transmittance of the Spirit through the Apostles takes place through ordination, modeled on the ordination of Timothy: "For this reason, I remind you to stir into flame the gift of God that you have through the imposition of my hands."[25] Further: [26] "Take as your norm the sound words that you heard from me, in the faith and love that are in Christ Jesus. Guard this rich trust with the help of the holy Spirit that dwells within us."[27] This is the basis for the ordination of the elders (presbyters) in Orthodox and Catholic churches and serves as a sure foundation for administering the sacraments of the Eucharist (Holy Communion), Confirmation (possibly Baptism with the Holy Spirit), Anointing of the Sick and Absolution after Confession. It should be added that the act of ordination is reserved for bishops, and each bishop sits on the chair of his predecessor. Today, auxiliary bishops who do not administer a bishopric receive the chair of a bishop whose bishopric does not even exist anymore. This aspect of episcopal ordination is hardly ever stressed anymore. It should also be pointed out that though the Bishop of Rome, the pope, is ordained as a bishop, he only receives his special position as pope because the bishop chair on which he sits was once the chair of the Apostle Peter. Besides, it is an open question whether only a bishop can ordain a priest or whether another priest may do so also. Certain popes endowed certain priests with the right to ordain priests.[28] The privileges of bishops might only be determined by canon law, or perhaps also by their special position. For confirmation, too, there needs to be a bishop or perhaps a priest who has been appointed by the bishop as his representative, because confirmation is an act that stands in relation to a certain bishopric. The reason it is not quite clear what an ordained person is entitled to do is that there is a difference between the *successio materialis* (spiritual ordainment) and the *successio formalis* (ecclesiastical law),[29] and the *successio formalis* might only have limited applicability. My personal conviction is that everyone can pass on what he has received from the Holy Spirit, which would mean that, as far as the *successio materialis* is concerned (apart from the seat), there is no difference between bishop and priest.[30]

Ordination has created a spiritual protection for the church, transmitting the Holy Spirit and creating a barrier against evil and mixed spirits. It should be noted, however, that neither baptism nor marriage requires ordination.

The attacks by evil spirits in the course of church history can be traced as follows:

Eusebius (260/64–339/40), the father of church history, already noted that, in the second century, internal issues of heresies and divisions were a much greater threat to Christianity than the outer threat of persecution.[31] The Holy Spirit who hovers over the earth has been mixed with the evil spirits who reside there. Although they do not succeed in destroying the church, as the church is protected, there are many people who develop an errant faith, which probably has something to do with the lacking protection of faith and baptism. What remains unchallenged are the four sacraments that are dependent on the transmittance of the Spirit through the Apostles and are being passed on by an ordained elder (presbyter). This is primarily the Eucharist (Holy Communion), but Confirmation is also important for the transmittance of the Holy Spirit, as well as the Anointing of the Sick, either healing the anointed through the gift of healing, strengthening them in enduring their sickness or helping them to die a good death. Finally, there is Absolution after Confession, which cancels grave sins that separated the person from God. As already mentioned, what is not secured by the apostolicity of the church are baptism and marriage, neither of which is transmitted through anointed elders. Baptism is the work of the baptizand who believes and wants to be baptized.[32] The person who conducts the baptism does not even have to be baptized himself,[33] and it is sufficient for the baptizand to have made the decision to get baptized, even if he dies before he can actually get baptized (the so-called "baptism of desire").[34] Neither does a martyr actually have to be baptized (the so-called "blood baptism").[35] When it comes to marriage, it is the marriage partners who administer the sacrament to each other, and it is an open question whether this depends on the faith of the receiver or the faith of the giver. Unsurprisingly, the kind of faith that has been distorted by evil spirits mostly affects believing laypersons and their marriages.

(1) The breaking away of Jewish believers, which started happening especially after the death (martyrdom) of James in Jerusalem (A.D. 62/63), cannot necessarily be counted as the effect of evil spirits, even though such groups often denied the divinity of Christ (Ebionites, Nazarites, Elcesaites as well as Cerinth, against which, according to Irenaeus, the Apostle John is supposed to have written his Gospel).[36]

(2) Gnosticism is a different matter, which goes back to pagan teachings[37] and which already the Apostle Paul strongly opposed.[38] The bases for Gnosticism are especially the mystery cults that promised their initiates access to the beyond. We have quoted a text from this stream of thought.[39] These were cults that offered experiences with the beyond, meaning that the initiates communicated with evil spirits. These teachings, though originally pagan, tried to appropriate aspects of the Christian faith. Gnosticism advocates a dualism that completely separates the highest god from the material world below. "Redemption" consists of a person being freed from the darkness of the material world, entering the divine light. Christ, accordingly, is seen as a purely spiritual being that only *appeared* to take on a body through Jesus of Nazareth. In reality, he could not possibly suffer and die on the cross. The death on the cross thus has no redemptive meaning; only the teaching of the right knowledge is important. Christ, according to Gnostics, left us a double revelation: a

lower revelation that is being proclaimed in the Holy Scriptures and the mainline church, and a higher, secret revelation that is entrusted to only a few elect, that is, the Gnostics.[40]

Via Manichaeism, this teaching survived into medieval times through sects such as the Pauleans, Bogomiles and the Cathari. Even in modern times, aspects of it can still be found in Spiritism, theosophy, the anthroposophy of Steiner, etc.

(3) Manichaeism goes back to the Persian Mani (215–273) who advocated a stark dualism. In a constant battle between light and darkness, between good and evil, the main objective is to overcome evil. This teaching, too, posed a danger to the Christian faith by appropriating certain Christian elements. Before he was baptized, even Augustine had succumbed to its teachings.

(4) For a time in the second century, Marcionism[42] was the most dangerous competitor of the Christian church. Marcion was the son of the bishop of Sinope at the Black Sea, born in 85. He, too, preached a stark dualism. He rejected the Old Testament. Yahwe, he said, was the wrathful god of evil. For him, too, the good God Christ only appeared to have a body and only appeared to have died. Excommunicated by the church in Rome, Marcion founded his own church, which was well organized and, for a number of years in the second century, was the most dangerous competition of the Christian mainline church.

(5) Around ca. 170, the "abstainers" (Encratites) found broad appeal. These, too, though embracing Christian dogma, were extremely ascetic and opposed to the physical body. They demanded that every Christian practice complete abstinence from meat, wine, and marriage.[43]

(6) Finally, Montanism[44] should also be mentioned, which was advocated by a former Cybele priest. Like the other heretics, he demanded strict asceticism and said that Christians ought to seek martyrdom. The most significant point, however, is that Montanus claimed to have been led by the Spirit, and, together with two women named Priscilla and Maximilla, he claimed to have had prophetic insights and revelations. In northern Africa, even Tertullian succumbed to Montanism. This was the movement that caused the church in the second half of the second century to largely abandon the gifts of the Holy Spirit.

Evil spirits were rejected together with the Holy Spirit. This was the protection in the wilderness. Instead of operating in the gifts of the Spirit, the principle of apostolic tradition was set down in detail, the canon of the Holy Scriptures was determined and there were joint decisions made by bishops. After the Constantinian shift, this climaxed in the Council of Nicaea, making the church strongly dogmatic.

C. The Problem of Baptism

As already pointed out, baptism is valid if the person to be baptized has faith and, of course, the desire to get baptized. "Whoever believes and is baptized will be saved."[45] The person conducting the baptism does not have to be ordained. In fact, he can even be an unbaptized unbeliever. It is enough that he intends to do what the church does.[46] This means that the baptism of small children is definitely a problem. There is no evidence that infant baptism existed in the early church. The reference that that a person was baptized together with his household[47] does not necessarily mean that small children were among those baptized. The household might have simply consisted of grown children and slaves. Even in that case, it remains an open question whether the members of the household had the necessary faith and desire to be baptized. There was a practice among Jews to circumcise small children and baptize converts together with their children prior to circumcision. But this, too, does not help us, as this was a baptism of cleansing such as John the Baptist practiced, not the baptism that symbolized death and resurrection. It is noteworthy that the Greek Orthodox Church only baptized children in connection with Confirmation and First Communion. This is why these three sacraments are called the initiation sacraments, which would otherwise not be the case for the Eucharist. In the Eastern Church, it was apparently believed that baptism was made more valid by connecting it to two sacraments administered by an ordained priest. In the Latin Catholic Western Church, children seemed to have been baptized much less often in the beginning. Even the Bible translator Hieronymus (347–420), who had Christian parents, was not baptized as a child but only decided to get baptized when he was twenty years old. It is worth mentioning that some older churches in Italy have a baptistery with a baptismal font that was clearly meant for adults.

Infant baptism seems to have been the result of the Christian faith being enforced by the state. This began in antiquity with Emperor Theodosius I (347–395), who outlawed paganism. But it was especially among the Germanic tribes that this was continued, where people were simply commanded by the leading aristocracy to become Christians. The Goths and Vandals, and originally also the Franks, all converted to Arianism in order to avoid being subject to the Roman Empire. Later, the Franks converted to Catholicism in order to be able to rule over Catholic Gaul, after which they forced the pagan Saxons to become Catholic as well. Harald Bluetooth, King of Denmark and later also of Norway, was baptized in 960 and accepted help from the church in order to unite Denmark. On All Saints' Day in 985 or 986, he died from an arrow wound inflicted on him by pagan enemies. This is why he is honored as a saint. Luther wanted to reintroduce baptism of adults, but due to the peasant revolts, he held onto infant baptism in order to please the aristocracy. The aristocracy liked to have Christian subjects because they could use the idea of the tithe in the Bible to demand the tenth of their income for themselves. It was only in the course of the French Revolution that, influenced by Rousseau, a different (democratic) basis for state power was accepted, and state and church were clearly separated, since the state had initially become openly atheistic. This is why adult baptism among non-state churches is no longer a political threat.

Today, the Catholic Church bases its practice of infant baptism on two factors: First of all, the sequence of the different stages in one's spiritual development are said to be inconsequential. This means that baptism can occur before someone actually believes. Of course, faith is supposed to grow as the child grows. That is why the children say a creed at their First Communion, which is done today when the children are about nine years old, as well as at Confirmation, when they are between sixteen and eighteen. In addition, there is a "renewal of baptism" for the whole congregation during Easter mass. The congregation says the creed and, as a reminder of their baptism, is sprinkled with holy water. What would be appropriate on this occasion would also be that the people give their agreement to the baptism they received. In addition, there is still a certain amount of collectivism among the Catholic Church when it comes to the faith. A child is seen as automatically becoming a believer at the appropriate age, simply due to the faith of its parents, its godparents and the entire church by which it is surrounded. This kind of influence starts through the mother before the child is even born. That is why the parents and godparents speak the creed on behalf of the infant before it is baptized. This is in line with the liturgy, in which it says, among other things, "Do not look on our sins but on the faith of your church." After the Second Vatican Council, some Catholics started to refuse baptism if the child's parents were unbelievers, but this trend quickly stopped. Considering the current state of the church, it would probably be better to return to baptism of adults. This would pose no problem even in case when a child dies unexpectedly, since raising the child in the faith, with the goal of later baptism, could qualify as a "baptism of desire."[48] According to Catholic doctrine, after all, those who declared their intention of getting baptized and are preparing for it are saved even if they die before the baptism.

D. The Time of the Woman in the Wilderness

In Revelation 12:6, it says that the woman is being taken care of in the wilderness for "twelve hundred and sixty days." From this it follows that this situation of the church comes to an end at some point. It is not quite clear when this end is reached, since the numbers in the Book of Revelation are symbolic in character. This becomes obvious once we realize that this same "time" is given twice more, but in different ways: (1) In Revelation 12:14: "A year, two years, and a half-year." (2) In Revelation 13:5: "Forty-two months." Arithmetically, these numbers are the same:

$3\frac{1}{2} \times 12 \times 30 = 1260$ (days)
$3\frac{1}{2}$ (years of 12×30 days)
$3\frac{1}{2} \times 12 = 42$ (months of 30 days)

If we interpret these numbers symbolically, we notice that 3½ is half of 7, and 7 is the number of fullness. Half of it is the opposite, referring to the fact that the situation of the woman in the wilderness comes to an end. The number 12 refers to the Apostles, and 30 can be interpreted as 3 x 10, which would be a reference to God (3) and his 10 Commandments, since the Lord did not come to abolish the Law but to fulfill it.

The prophecy in Joel,[49] too, suggests that the time of the woman in the wilderness would come to an end at some point. This means that there would again be believers who live outside of the wilderness, who receive the Holy Spirit through his free movement, and it is explicitly stated that women, maidservants and menservants etc. would receive the Holy Spirit as well.

E. What Can the Church Expect after the Time in the Wilderness?

Revelation also gives a picture of what happens to the church at the end of the wilderness time:

Then I looked and there was the Lamb standing on Mount Zion, and with him a hundred and forty-four thousand who had his name and his Father's name written on their foreheads. I heard a sound from heaven like the sound of rushing water or a loud peal of thunder. The sound I heard was like that of harpists playing their harps. They were singing (what seemed to be) a new hymn before the throne, before the four living creatures and the elders. No one could learn this hymn except the hundred and forty-four thousand who had been ransomed from the earth. These are they who were not defiled with women; they are virgins and these are the ones who follow the Lamb wherever he goes. They have been ransomed as the firstfruits of the human race for God and the Lamb. On their lips no deceit has been found; they are unblemished.[50]

The woman in the wilderness (Rev 12) with the twelve stars on her head corresponds to the 144,000 who are with the Lamb on Mount Zion singing a new song, accompanied by the sound of a harp from heaven (Rev 12). Both are pictures of a church that can be called apostolic. In the case of the woman, the apostolicity consists of the twelve Apostles—the stars on her head—who pass on the blessing of the Holy Spirit to certain people in later generations. In the case of the 144,000, it is people who took in and passed on what the Apostles had said and written. 144 is 12 times 12, and it is an old Egyptian idea that a square number is a way of generalizing something. Hence, a triad was the symbol for every single god—not because they believed in the Trinity but because, according to Egyptian grammar, it signified not only plurality but also infinity.[51] When an Egyptian mentioned the gods of his city, he referred to the holy "nineness," even if it was not exactly nine gods.[52] Accordingly, the number for the Pharaoh—who was believed to be both a man and the son of a god—was 5, consisting of 3 for a god and 4 for the world, but put together from these generalizations, that is, from the square numbers: $3^2 + 4^2 = 5^2$. Pythagoras, the Greek philosopher, went to Egypt to be instructed there, and he brought the calculations for the sides of an orthogonal triangle home with him. Today, we only take the mathematical aspect from him, and, unfortunately, some Evangelicals interpret the numbers in the Bible according to this modern, intellectual understanding. In contrast, the number for the God-man Jesus Christ is also 5, since he has five wounds, and the number of the ancient patriarchies was 5 as well (Antioch, Alexandria, Constantinople, Jerusalem and Rome for the Occident). I would like to add that the Bible itself shows that the Israelites adopted some things from the Egyptians, taking things from Egypt with them. This does not only follow from Moses' education in Pharaoh's family but also from the fact that God instructed the Israelites to ask the Eygptians for "silver and gold articles" to take with them, which the Fathers of the Church called the *spolia Aegyptorum.*[53] For the Israelites higher up in rank, this had a greater significance. In the case of Moses, it says in this connection explicitly: "Moses himself was very highly regarded by Pharaoh's servants and the people in the land of Egypt."

After this little excursus, let us continue with the 144,000: It says that they have been ransomed, meaning ransomed from sin, and they have not been defiled with women. The latter, one should not take literally; rather, it means that they did not follow the ways of the world and, in particular, did not subject themselves to the influence of people who were driven by evil spirits. As we shall see, the 144,000 are, in fact, the Pentecostal churches for whom the apostolic ordination has no meaning, since the

Spirit blows where it wills. In some countries, they suffer persecution, but they have renounced the world. The persecution is pictured in Revelation 13.

F. Joachim of Fiore

The arrival of the New Time and the New Song after or beside the church as a woman in the wilderness was actually predicted in the thirteenth century, albeit without referring to the details in the Book of Revelation. Especially Joachim of Fiore gave a very well-founded prophecy.[54] The son of a notary of the Norman royal court, Joachim of Fiore was born around the year 1135 in Celico, near Cosenza, in the Calabria region of southern Italy. He had connections to Cistercian monasteries and, for a considerable time, served as the abbot of the monastery Corazzo. In 1184, he asked the pope to discharge him from this office, which enabled him to found a new religious order in the Sila Mountains: the Florians with their mother monastery in San Giovanni. He died in 1202.

Joachim of Fiore's theory of history can be summed up as follows:

First of all, there are three different ages: the age of the Father, the age of the Son, and the age of the Holy Spirit. The age of the Father lasted from Abraham until the father of John the Baptist.

The first two ages have the same length and correspond to each other in their different phases. According to Matthew, the age of the Father lasts forty-two generations.[55] Joachim counts one generation as lasting thirty years, which leads him to a period of 1260 years. This, in his view, is also the length of the age of the Son, meaning that the age of the Holy Spirit would follow after that.

It is interesting that this is the same number as that of the woman in the wilderness. But this number by Joachim must be taken with some reservation, since his length of a generation can only be seen as an average. Abraham, for instance, was much older when his son Isaac was born. Of course, Joachim knew that, and he also taught that one period of time could overlap with the next. Nevertheless, he expected an important shift for the church in the thirteenth century.

Joachim of Fiore says that though he did not receive an inspiration about the length of the three ages, he did receive one regarding the reasoning behind the analogy. He tells the story of how he woke up during Easter vigil, and, by the grace of the Holy Spirit, received insight into the Holy Scriptures, but no prophecy.[56] Personally, I am of the opinion that it was precisely the other way around. The twelfth, thirteenth and fourteenth centuries are clearly marked by the start of a new age, but his theory of the three ages is not even biblical.

It might be possible to call the time of the Israelites the age of the Father, although, even during that time, the Holy Spirit is often active, and there are also repeated pointers to the Son.

If we grant that this was the age of the Father, it might be more appropriate, however, to see Noah rather than Abraham as its beginning. And the age of the Son would have to start not with the father of John the Baptist but either with Jesus' birth or, rather, with the Annunciation to Mary. Either way, the age of the Son ended with his Ascension. Nine days later was Pentecost, which means that the age of the Holy Spirit already started, and there is no real end to that age but rather a culmination in the age of all three Persons with the return of Christ and the renewed calling of the Israelites, the latter of which could be assigned to the Father. However, we do not know the length of the age of the Spirit before the return of Christ.[57]

The Bible says that God created the world in six "days" and that he rested on the seventh "day." But his rest found an end with the first coming of Jesus Christ, which had a precursor in the history of the Israelites. In other words, Christ brought the eighth "day" that has no end. The word *day* is used here in a figurative sense, since God created both day and night on the first "day."

Without a doubt, the age of the Spirit started with Pentecost. But it is like the Jewish liturgical day: it begins the night before at sunset, and it gets dark before the night turns into bright day. It is the same way with the eighth day: the Spirit came on Pentecost, leading to the time of the Apostles, after which it immediately became "dark" until the time that Joachim predicted. It is also possible to see this in terms of former and latter rains, like Joel did.[58]

Finally, one should also take into account that with the return of Christ and the conversion of the Israelites—and during the time leading up to it—the working of the Spirit becomes stronger too.

But before we come to that point, we should talk about the timeframe that Joachim had in mind. Let us first look at what Joachim predicted about the age of the Spirit and then at what actually happened after his death.

(a) The (Believing) People

Spiritually speaking, what is central after the time of Joachim is "contemplation" as practiced, for instance, by John of the Cross. Joachim of Fiore put it like this: people study and write, not read.[59]

"People no longer need written documents but themselves have access to the truth. The Spirit dwells supernaturally inside the believers and turns their life into a spiritual one."[60] This contrast might be compared to the difference between a theological seminary or university on the one hand and a more spiritually oriented Bible school on the other hand. It is reminiscent of what was said of Moses (among others): he experienced God not in pictures or through words but eye to eye.[61] (The translation "face to face" is not clear enough.) If you look someone in the eye in this way, you do not look at whether their eyes are blue or brown. Rather, you look into their heart. In the New Testament, it says that we are in God and God is in us, which expresses the same kind of relationship.

Furthermore, the people during the age of the Spirit are moved by the love of God, hence forming a community of love.[62] The prophecy that there would be no more war is going to come true, Joachim says. The Spirit is not a Spirit of forgiving, as there is no more sin because the Son Jesus is forgiving.[63] This is why the sin against the Holy Spirit cannot be forgiven.[64]

People do not marry and produce no children, neither do they work. Nevertheless, the age of the Spirit is supposed to last for several generations. This reminds one of the statement by the Apostle Paul to the effect that people could have as though they did not have. According to Joachim, laypersons, too, could be monks in a spiritual sense.[65]

These predictions mix the age of the Spirit with the kingdom that is to last for a thousand years after the return of Christ.[66] Unsurprisingly, many people who based their views on Joachim advocated a chiliasm that was quite this-worldly, expecting it to arrive before the return of Christ.

One can object to Joachim that the age of the Spirit prior to the return of Christ is not at all free from war and work, and that there also have to be marriages, even though the Adversary would like to restructure human sexuality. Persecution of Christians, too, is an essential element of this time.

In my assessment, a typical example for the age of the Spirit is the deacon Stephen who, though he was stoned to death, saw the heavens open and, we can surmise, experienced great joy about what he beheld. He is followed by all martyrs who make the cross of Christ real in their own time and, by doing so, drive away evil spirits.

Finally, Joachim also mentioned that the time of the Spirit would be marked by *gaudium, laudare, psallere*. This springs from the kingdom of God, especially to the benefit of the martyrs.[67]

(b) The Clergy

During the time of the Spirit, the clergy is supposed to dissolve. There are no more priests and bishops. The hierarchy of Catholicism disappears.[68] This applies first to the structure of the Church but then also to the sacraments, which, after all, are dependent on ordained priests.

(c) The Sacraments

The sacraments turn into something "spiritual." Instead of water baptism, there is the baptism with the Holy Spirit and fire.[69] The Greek *mysterion* comes to the fore.[70] Even today, we often talk about the primal sacrament that is the basis of all other sacraments. Particularly noteworthy is the change of the Eucharist. This is hinted at in the Gospel of John. Even though John does mention the "breaking of bread" in his account of the Last Supper before the crucifixion, he does not go into detail, as the other Gospel authors do.[71] Instead, he mentions that Jesus already talked at a much earlier point about people needing to eat his body and drink his blood.[72] There, the consequences are laid out in stark detail. However, Jesus does not say how exactly the eating of his body and drinking of his blood is to happen. According to Joachim, it has to happen in a spiritual manner.

(d) The Pope

Joachim does not unequivocally answer the question of whether there will still be a pope. At one time, he says that the people of the saints (*populous sanctorum*) would take the place of the pope.[73] There is also talk of an "angel pope."[74] However, much more often, Joachim only speaks of the returning Elijah. At other times, he speaks of the angel at the rising of the sun in Revelation.[75]

Joachim of Fiore was not at all neglected or even rejected by the Catholic Church, having been personally acquainted with four succeeding popes (1181–1198).[76] At the commission of three of these popes, Joachim wrote three of his greatest works, which were later edited in the sixteenth century. He explicitly submitted these works to the approval of the pope.[77] After his death, too, Joachim was in favor with the curia. The order he founded received generous gifts from the popes.[78]

Pope Clement III (1187-91) urged Joachim in a letter to complete his first two major works that the pope's predecessors had asked him to begin. On the other hand, the letter closes with quite a strong warning to keep the works hidden. Joachim, too, in the prologue to his work, prohibited the members of his order from spreading his writings.[79] Different interpretations are possible to make sense of this conduct.[80] The fact is that Joachim was condemned because of his critique of the teaching on the Trinity by Peter Lombard, which, however, did not touch the essential points of his own teaching on the age of the Spirit. Joachim opposed the Trinitarian doctrine of Peter Lombard (Bishop of Paris from 1159–1160), whose *Books of Sentences* became a foundational textbook on dogma on which all the Scholastics since the thirteenth century commented. Due to his polemic against Lombard, Joachim was declared as heretical after his death during the Fourth Lateran Council in 1215.[81]

Even though Joachim of Fiore predicted profound changes in the church, he adhered clearly to the rule of the church that existed in his own time, since he thought that the changes would only take full effect in

1260, and he died in 1202. However, as already mentioned, he was of the opinion that there was some overlap of the different ages and that the age of the Spirit had already started with Benedict of Nursia and the Benedictine Order.

Accordingly, there had to be further signs of the coming changes. I do not know whether one could count the charismatic personalities of Hugh of St. Victor (1097–1141) and Bernhard of Clairvaux (1090–1153), who were also filled by the free blowing of the Spirit. We do know, however, that there were elements in the church that went against the rules of the time. There were sectarians who moved into a similar direction that Joachim had predicted. Of particular note is Hugo Speroni, a Lombardic jurist who was consul in Piacenza from 1164 to 1171.[82] He voiced sharp criticism of the clergy, as well as of infant baptism, adoration of the cross and images, feasts of the saints, rules for fasting, righteousness by works, and externalization of Christian worship, since he believed in the preeminence of the "inner man" who was sanctified through the love of Christ. And he was not alone in his critique; rejection of the administration of sacraments through unworthy priests was widespread.

Of even greater significance was Catharism.[83] The Cathari moved about without possessions and practiced daily "breaking of bread" instead of mass with its Holy Communion. Also, instead of conducting water baptisms, they laid their hands on believers to baptize them "with the Spirit" (in accordance with Acts 8:17). They gave up eating meat, never swore an oath and rejected marriage. Using the Greek word *kathari*, they called themselves "the pure," which is probably the origin of the German word for heretic, *Ketzer*. Eventually, the Cathari were influenced from the East by the sect of the Bogomiles, who had a radically dualistic worldview. The degree to which this sect was also influenced by a belief in the age of the Spirit is hard to say. It is not my concern here to speak of the political problems of such sectarian movements, such as the Albigensian wars, which played an important role for the Cathari.[84]

A final example is the Waldensians and Humiliati.[85] The Waldensians were founded after 1173 by a rich merchant from Lyon named Valdes. He asked to have the Gospels, the Psalter and other parts of the Bible translated for him. Moved by what he read, he gave everything he had to the poor and, now a poor beggar, went about barefoot preaching the gospel. The archbishop prohibited him from preaching on the street and public squares, but he soon had other people who joined him. Not wanting to be heretics, they preached against the heresies of the Cathari as well as against the deplorable conduct of the clergy. They turned to the curia for help against the archbishop, appearing in 1179 on the Third Lateral Council. The pope is said to have praised their commitment to poverty, which caused him to embrace Valdes. Nevertheless, the Waldensians were forbidden to preach without a special commission by the bishop, a prohibition which they did not keep. A kind of mendicant order arose among them. But it was only when they were excommunicated that they began to reject certain dogmas. For example, the question whether a priest acted in a worthy manner seemed more important to them than the question whether he was ordained. Soon, even though they were laypeople, they came to conclude that they, too, had the right to conduct baptisms, to give each other absolution, receive Communion among themselves and even elect their own bishops. It is probably not too much to say that the rejection by the church caused the Waldensians to open themselves to a new experience of the Spirit, an experience that did not come about through ordination but through the pious life of laypeople.

The Humiliati were similar, even though they did not live as beggars but rather as working people, thus forming a kind of Third Order. It is interesting to note that Pope Innocent III (1198-1216) soon realized that it was problematic to declare them as heretics. In 1201, the Humiliati were recognized as a pious lay community, even allowing them to preach, though not about articles of faith and the sacraments. Some Waldensians, too, were admitted back into the Church.

Chapter 2

The Time after Joachim of Fiore

A. After Joachim of Fiore—the Franciscans

Fiorism had the most marked influence on the Franciscan Order, which came into being shortly after the death of Joachim of Fiore. In my depiction of this order, I follow closely what Walter Nigg wrote in his book *Das ewige Reich* ("The Eternal Kingdom").[86] The order was split into two different groups with different orientations: the Conventuals, who toned down the lack of possessions that Francis (1181/82–1226) desired. Although the individual members were required to be propertyless, this did not apply to the order as a whole. Obedience was the most important duty. The church leadership favored this direction. Then there were the Spirituals, who thought that the order, too, should be poor, which was in line with the will of Francis himself. The clash between these two groups intensified through the influence of Joachim of Fiore's teachings. In 1241, a fleeing abbot brought all of Joachim's writings to the Franciscan monastery in Pisa. On every page, the Franciscans found what seemed like descriptions of themselves, which poured oil on the fire of their differences.[87]

This is how Walter Nigg describes the situation:[88] "Celano reports that Francis himself had talked to his brothers about the 'eternal kingdom' and had proclaimed the kingdom of God during his travels on foot (Celano ch. 12 & 23). This was the message from which his indescribable joy flowed that shone through all his ecstatic actions. It was obvious to others that he thought of himself as a new evangelist who lived in the last days, bringing unexpected joy to the people of the world. This view was increased by his Spiritual disciples to the point that his person was raised almost to a similar importance for salvation history as

Christ himself. Even Bonaventura was not able to completely distance himself from this rather overblown interpretation of Francis, saying in his official biography of Francis, 'Filled by a prophetic spirit, entrusted with the mission of an angel, becoming aflame in the sepharic glow, it is clear from the course of his life that he came in the spirit and power of Elijah.'[89] The mysterious word of the Revelation of John, which Christendom had never understood before—'I saw another angel come up from the East, holding the seal of the living God'[90]—suddenly revealed its meaning by being applied to Francis. The Spirituals saw Francis as the world-historical figure that was the fulfillment of the new age that Joachim had predicted. In Francis, they saw the answer to the question raised by Joachim. Peter John Olivi's commentary on the Apocalypse, which became the favorite book of the Spirituals, applies Joachim's schema to Francis, who, according to him, 'was truly the angel who opened the sixth seal.'"[91]

In line with their chiliasm, people at the time also expected the Antichrist to arrive. Most of them identified him as Emperor Frederick II, which caused a major blow when he died in 1250, before the date of the beginning of the age of the Spirit in 1260. Also, when 1260 came, nothing happened. Then there was the victory of the Ghibellines over the Welfs at Montaperto, as well as the procession of the flagellants of Perugia. As a final blow, the papacy turned against them, particularly John XXII, the richest pope for as long as anyone could remember, causing them to expect the "angel pope" who was supposed to come.

At least, Hildegard of Bingen[92] prophesied a holy end time for the time of Francis, which I understand to refer to his spirituality and the replacement of crusades by true evangelism among the Muslims.[93]

B. The Hussites

John Huss (1370–1415), a Czech born in Southern Bohemia, was influenced by the ideas of the Englishman John Wycliffe (ca. 1320-84).[94] Wycliffe opposed the wealth of the prelacy of the church, rejecting its hierarchy and advocating a spiritual "church of the predestined" that should live in apostolic poverty. This means that he, too, envisioned a church that was not dependent on top-down ordination but on the free blowing of the Spirit. The church, in his view, should only have room for people who were predestined to live in a state of grace. No one who committed a deadly sin could have a leading position in the church or in the state. The sacraments, accordingly, did not have any significance.

Huss defended this view and met with great applause among his Czech audience, in part because the critique of the prelature ruling over Bohemia appealed to their national sentiments, since the prelature mostly consisted of Germans. At the Council of Constance in 1415, Huss ended up being sentenced to death by burning, since he did not even want to distance himself from a false interpretation of his statements.

The real spread of the Hussites only started after the death of Huss, as his death caused great indignation among the Czechs.[95] The political dimension of the movement was not only directed against the Germans but also by the impoverished lower urban classes and the peasants against the ruling classes. The desire for social change was combined with religious ideas.

During Easter 1419, Hussite clergy erected a tent on a hill in Southern Bohemia, conducting a service in the Czech language. They felt like the disciples on Mount Tabor during Jesus' transfiguration when Peter wanted to build a tent.[96] They even called the hill Tabor, creating a euphoric atmosphere. Transfiguration, not the chalice, was their symbol. The celebration became quite orgiastic. Under the leadership of the priest Huska and the peasant Niklas, a chiliastic hope arose. The Hussites began to expect that the world would end in February 1420, that is, the end of the time of grace and the beginning of the time of retaliation against evil people. "People hostile to the divine law have to be destroyed through fire and sword, like Sodom was made level through fire, except for five cities, in accordance with Isaiah 19:18. The Taborites will be the ones executing the just judgment. Christ will be neither a king, ruler nor subject on the earth, and all tributes and taxes will cease. No one will force anyone else into anything, because everyone will be equal as brothers and sisters." God himself would be king. "The churches are to be torn down and human knowledge is to be put to the side. Baptism and Communion no longer have any purpose. Even the Bible has become superfluous, since the law of God has been written into the hearts of everyone. Children will be born without pain and will never die. The dead will rise. A kind of Christian communism comes into being. Everyone sells everything they have, sharing everything. Private property is a deadly sin. Peasants plunder castles and monasteries. Churches are being destroyed. Pope Martin V calls for a crusade against the Hussites. In vain. Finally, however, the movement dies by itself. It has no religious leader. Then comes the Plague—killing fifty percent of the Occident—and the armies of the Turks; a feud among the aristocracy—a general sense of doom—and finally the movements of the flagellants (1430–1530).“

Centuries later, a more extreme form of this conception of the millennial kingdom was born: communism,[97] which replaced religious sentiments with intellectual sentiments. The movement started with the utopias of Saint-Simon, Fourier, and Owen, and became something of a science with Kant, Fichte, and particularly Hegel.[98] Early socialism (especially that of Wilhelm Weitling[99]) was chiliastic, but it expected the kingdom of God to come in a this-worldly manner. This is also true of religious socialism, which arose later, founded by Christoph Blumhardt d.J.[100] In the communism of the Jew Karl Marx, chiliasm was only a subconscious contributor.[101] Officially, he was a materialist and an atheist, thus being a kindred spirit of Nietzsche.[102] Out of the catastrophe of revolution (and the socialist-proletarian dictatorship), Marx thought, the salvation of communism would arise.[103] And once more it was a Slavic people that advocated this kind of chiliasm, this time not primarily the Czech but the Russians.[104] It was a secularized chiliasm, a perverted kind of messianism, a substitute for religion.[105]

It is worthwhile making clear at this point what the Bible actually says about the second coming of Christ:

The basis is John's Revelation (Rev 20:1–6): "Then I saw an angel come down from heaven, holding in his hand the key to the abyss and a heavy chain. He seized the dragon, the ancient *serpent*, which is the *Devil or Satan*, and tied it up for a thousand years and threw it into the abyss, which he locked over it and sealed, so that it could no longer lead the nations astray until the thousand years are completed. After this, it is to be released for a short time. *Then I saw thrones*; those who *sat on them were entrusted with judgment*. I also saw the souls of those who had been beheaded for their witness to Jesus and for the word of God, and who had not worshiped the beast or its image nor had accepted its mark on their foreheads or hands. They came to life and they reigned with Christ for a thousand years. The rest of the dead did not come to life until the thousand years were over. This is the first resurrection. Blessed and holy is the one who shares in the first resurrection. The second death has no power over these; they will be *priests* of God and of Christ, and they will reign with him for (the) thousand years." It is possible that Revelation 1:7 also refers to this first resurrection: "*Behold, he is coming amid the clouds*, and every eye will see him, *even those who pierced him.* All the peoples of the earth *will lament him.* Yes. Amen." As well as Romans 11:25-32 about the Jews: "I do not want you to be unaware of this mystery, brothers, so that you will not become wise (in) your own estimation: a hardening has come upon Israel in part, until the full number of the Gentiles comes in, and thus all Israel will be saved …" etc. Finally, First Corinthians 15:20-58 should be taken into consideration, especially: "… but each one in proper order: Christ the firstfruits; then, at his coming, those who belong to Christ; then comes the end, when he hands over the kingdom to his God and Father, when he has destroyed every sovereignty and every authority and power." Apart from these, there are also some prophecies in the Old Testament that mostly relate to the Israelites.

During the millennial reign of Christ, sin will disappear. Augustine, in particular, applied the prophecies of the millennial kingdom to the heart of the believer, denoting their sanctification. According to this view, the millennial kingdom has already come through the rise of the church. Since Augustine, this is the view that predominates in the Catholic Church. Of course, it is true that the kingdom has come in the hearts of the believers. Paul, after all, said, "I live, no longer I, but Christ lives in me." However, this does not preclude the possibility that there will also be a more encompassing second coming of Christ, one that will be of special significance for the Jews.

The following points regarding the millennial kingdom are essential:

It will come with the second coming of Christ, who will return in the way in which he went, that is, in his "resurrection body."[106]

The Lord will come back when "the full number of the Gentiles comes in" … "until the times of the Gentiles are fulfilled."[107]

Before the second coming of the Lord, there will be "signs in the sun, the moon, and the stars, and on earth nations will be in dismay, perplexed by the roaring of the sea and the waves."[108] Also, there will be persecution of Christians, especially at the hands of the Antichrist.

The Jews (Israelites) will come to believe.[109]

When Christ comes back, all who belong to him are raised from the dead.[110] Being killed for one's faith does not seem to be a condition for this resurrection. Rather, it seems to refer to the fact that those who rise with Christ also have to die with him. After all, those who are still alive when he returns will be changed in an instant,[111] and this group definitely will not have died in a literal sense for their faith.

The bodies of those raised or transformed will be different than their mortal bodies, now being immortal.[112]

A kingdom of peace will be established.[113]

Obviously, all of this is far removed from what some chiliasts expected and tried to make happen.

C. Meister Eckhart and the Other Medieval Mystics

Walter Nigg (1903–1988) sees Meister Eckhart in connection with the predicted "kingdom of the Spirit." In his book *Das ewige Reich* ("The Eternal Kingdom"), he describes it as follows: "The incomparably bright-shining Meister Eckhart who, with brilliant boldness, ventured beyond the dogmatism of the church, gives a foretaste of a new age, as long as one understands the kingdom of the Spirit as truly spiritual."[114] Nigg points out that Eckhart was actually born in 1260, the year that Joachim of Fiore had predicted would be the beginning of the age of the spirit. This, however, might have only been an outward sign, since Joachim expected the different ages to overlap and since the thirty years he set for each generation is only an average number. Furthermore, we know now that the birth of Christ did not actually happen in the year zero.[115]

One of Meister Eckharts central teachings is that Jesus Christ was not just born once at Christmas but is born all the time anew in our soul. The above-mentioned book by Walter Nigg seems to have been one of his earliest. He wrote another book about Meister Eckhart, which appears to have been one of his last.[116] In it, he summarized Eckhart's teachings as follows: "The Son of God has to be born in man; only then does man come to experience the fullness of time."[117] The basis for the divine birth in man is the "spark of the soul." Eckhart expresses this in words that basically equate this spark with God himself. It was statements such as these that led to his condemnation by the Church. This, however, only happened after his death, which made it impossible for him to defend himself.[118] Uta Störmer-Caysa[119] has explained Eckhart's statements historically, concluding that his condemnation was unjustified. Still, Eckhart's works were destroyed and only rediscovered in the nineteenth century. However, his students Tauler and Suso continued his teaching, albeit in a changed form. Tauler had an influence on the Pietists. Luther, too, read him and viewed him positively.

Allow me to make a personal remark. It was during Easter in the Reformed Church that a sentence by G. W. F. Hegel—apparently guided by the Holy Spirit—made me a true believer and subsequently led me to receive the gift of speaking in tongues. Then, however, I read Eckhart and Tauler and decided to become a Catholic. Mysticism was something that was missing both in the Reformed Church and, of course, also in Hegel. At the time, I did not even know that there was such a thing as a Pentecostal movement.

Simplifying it a little, today I would say about the teachings of Eckhart that his idea of a spark of the soul was Marian. Mary is not only the perfect embodiment of the Israelite people but also of every soul. It is in her, and in every soul, that Christ is born. "Accidentally," I recently came across Eckhart's sermon "*Ave, gratia plena*," which he starts by citing Luke 1:28: "Hail, favored one! The Lord is with you," followed by Luke 1:35 (see also James 1:17 and Wisdom 18:15): "The holy Spirit will come upon you, and the power of the Most High will overshadow you." He goes on to explain that the reason the angel did not address the mother of God by her name was not only out of reverence for her but also because he did not address her alone, instead speaking to a great multitude of people: to every good soul that yearns for God. Furthermore, he says, "If Mary had not first given birth to God spiritually, she would have never given birth to him bodily." And then he says, "It is more important to God that he is born spiritually by every virgin—that is, by every good soul—than that he was born bodily by Mary."

If one takes this in, the Marian Rosary prayer gains a new meaning, because, by using the words of the angel, one calls on Mary in one's own soul, and this soul, taking on the role of Mary, gives birth to Jesus, walking with him though his stages of life, from his birth to his crucifixion and resurrection, ascension and the sending of his Spirit.[121] All of this happens within our soul.

Finally, Paul repeatedly pointed to the birth of Christ in us. For example: "I live, no longer I, but Christ lives in me."[122] For him, however, this does not happen through the birth of Jesus in our soul but through his crucifixion and resurrection, which is also something that happens in our soul. Augustine, too, spoke of the birth of Christ in our soul,[123] and particularly well-known is the saying of Angelus Silesius, who, like me, converted from Protestantism to Catholicism: "Christ could be born a thousand times, but all in vain until he is born in you!"[124]

Jesus Christ within us is like the effect of the Eucharist when we take Holy Communion or like the devotion to the Sacred Heart of Jesus when we give him our lives.

The second mystic, Johannes Tauler of Strasbourg (ca. 1300–1361), though influenced by Eckhart, avoided his more extreme statements that led to his condemnation. I will restrict my analysis to his Christmas sermon here, about the three births of Christ: the begetting of the Son through God the Father, the begetting of Jesus in Mary through the Holy Spirit, and, finally, "that God will truly be born every day and every hour in grace and love in every good soul."[125] In what follows, I will quote a few essential statements about what is required for this birth of Christ to take place in a person:

"The soul has three noble powers, wherein it is the true image of the blessed Trinity—memory [including the subconscious!], understanding and free will. Through these powers is the soul capable of comprehending and receiving God, taking part in all that God is, has and can bestow. Furthermore, it is able to look into eternity, for the soul is created between time and eternity; with its superior part it belongs to eternity, and with the inferior—the sensitive, animal powers—it belongs to time. Both the higher and lower powers of the soul wander away into time and into the fleeting things of time, and this is because of the kinship between its higher and lower powers. Very easy is it in this straying thus to go astray from eternity. If we would be born again with the divine birth, then we need to start back again."

"After that, there should a going-out, indeed a transcendence of ourselves and our own particular will and desires and working, and what needs to remain is only the naked, pure will of God, with nothing left of ours; not being, becoming or getting in any way in ourselves, but simply being for him and acceding to him in what is highest and nearest, thus enabling his working and birthing in ourselves without any hindrance."

Later, Protestants read Tauler, and he had a great impact on the Pietists.

The third mystic back then was Henry Suso (ca. 1295 – 1366) of Constance or Weinfelden in Thurgovia. In what follows, I mostly rely on Walter Nigg,[127] since it will be primarily biographical, but I will also refer to his works.[128]

Suso had his first mystical experience after a long time of inner emptiness.[129] "It was a sweetness that flowed out of eternal life in a quiet experience of present stillness." After this rapture it was as though he had come from a different world. He'd had glimpsed heaven. The reason for this grace was that he had made the firm resolve to end the emptiness inside of him, but, unlike some people today, he did not do so by taking drugs or seeking the nearness of death. After some time, he had a second experience.[130] In a vision, he saw a large group of youth coming toward him, "drawing him in to dance and sing joyfully about the Christ child." It was a mystical roundel that cannot be imagined in human terms. These mystical experiences led Suso to an ascetic lifestyle.[131] Deeply moved, Suso took a sharp slate pencil and stuck it pitilessly into his own flesh, right above the heart, scratching IHS[132] into his skin. His blood flowed. It was an act of dedicating himself fully to Christ. One is reminded of the Pietist Gerhard Tersteegen who wrote his dedication to Jesus with a pencil nib dipped in his own blood. It also bears a certain relation to the devotion to the Sacred Heart of Jesus, which we will come back to later. The main point of all of this is a Christian faith that truly comes from the heart.

Suso began his asceticism by giving up his favorite dishes and maintaining a deep silence. Sometimes he did not drink anything, even if he had great thirst.[133] He also wore a hair shirt and an iron chain on his clothes. He bound a cross covered in pointy nails across his back that caused him severe pain whenever he moved.

But, together with the pain, there was also a joy that grew in him.

Then, after sixteen years, on Pentecost, he had a vision: "Heavenly characters" told him that God no longer wanted his self-chastisement, which caused him to throw the tools of his self-torment into the Rhine. After that, he received the gift of minnesong in prose.[134] And he also discovered the divine in nature.[135]

Instead of his self-chastisement, he now experienced a spiritual suffering that occurred when others had a negative view of him.[136] But he said, "There is nothing more painful than suffering and nothing more joyful than having suffered. Suffering is a short song and a long delight."[137] Then: "Behold, the noble soul thrives on suffering like the rose thrives on the sweet dew of May. Suffering brings experience and a wise disposition. A person who has not suffered—what does he know?" And finally: "Why are you sitting there? Get up and sink into my suffering. That is how you overcome your own suffering!"[138]

For him, an important matter is also the acceptance of death. In the second part of his *Little Book of Eternal Wisdom*, chapter 21 is entitled "How to Learn to Die," which was distributed widely in late medieval times independently from the rest of the book.[139]

Something else that was essential for Suso was to have a basic attitude of "seclusion," (Abgeschiedenheit) as it was also for Eckhart.[140]

Chapter 3

Elements of Protestantism

A. Thomas Müntzer and His "Chiliasm"

My goal here is not to set forth all the theological differences between Thomistic Catholicism and modern Protestantism, which, in any case, would not be possible within the framework of this book. But I do want to point out that particularly within Lutheranism it is taught that justification by faith is confined to the legal standing of the believer before God, without thereby changing the soul of the believer, basically leaving his sinfulness the way it is, without working sanctification. However, I cannot quite follow the view that this was supposed to have been the opinion of Luther himself. In chapter 12 of his exposition *On the Freedom of a Christian*, he writes: "Faith does not turn the soul into something equal with the divine Word. By faith, the soul itself does not become full of every grace, free and blessed. Rather, faith unites the soul to Christ, as the wife to the husband; by which mystery, as the Apostle Paul teaches, Christ and the soul are made one flesh. Now if they are one flesh, and if a true marriage—nay, by far the most perfect of all marriages—is accomplished between them (for human marriages are but feeble types of this one great marriage), then it follows that all they have becomes theirs in common, as well good things as evil things; so that whatsoever Christ possesses, that the believing soul may take to itself and boast of as its own, and whatever belongs to the soul, that Christ claims as his. If we compare these possessions, we shall see how inestimable is the gain. … Who then can value highly enough these royal nuptials? Who can comprehend the riches of the glory of this grace that Christ, that rich and pious husband, takes as a wife a needy and impious harlot, redeeming her from all her evils, and supplying her with all his good things?" One does not have to stretch the text to interpret it as affirming inner holiness. This is particularly supported by Luther's comparison to the unity of the flesh, as well as his emphasis on joy.

Another point that needs to be highlighted is that Protestantism once more emphasized the priesthood of all believers, though the word *priest* can easily lead to misunderstandings. What it actually signifies is a word that comes from the Greek *presbyter*, meaning "elder." The Greek word for priest is *hiereus*. Hence, we speak of a "hierarchy," which literally means the rule of priests. Protestantism emphasized the priesthood of the believer in general terms, without, however, connecting this to the charismatic gifts of the Spirit. In the great statement of faith of the Catholic and Orthodox Church, the Nicene Creed, it says that the church is "apostolic." This is interpreted to mean that the elders receive their spiritual gifts through ordination in a historical line which leads back to an Apostle. This corresponds to the woman in the wilderness.[142] In his catechism, Luther uses the shorter creed, the so-called Apostolic Creed in which the church is not referred to as "apostolic."[143] The same is true of the Heidelberg Catechism.[144] Protestants today often recognize the Nicene Creed but give a different meaning to the word "apostolic" than the Catholic Church does. Of which more later.[145]

What is relevant for our topic is that Protestantism gave rise to movements that also emphasize the free blowing of the Spirit over all believers. The first person to mention in this connection is Thomas Müntzer (1490–1525). Wallmann[146] describes his orientation as follows: "What Müntzer learned from Luther fits together with medieval mysticism, especially Johannes Tauler's mysticism of suffering, as well as with chiliastic ideas and Taborist influences, to which he was exposed in the mining town of Zwickau and, after its spread from there (1521), also in Bohemia. The Word is understood as the inner Word that man hears when he detaches himself ascetically from all worldly shackles, experiencing the breakthrough of the Spirit in the 'wilderness of distress' and in 'poverty of spirit.' The outer word of the Scriptures, of sermons, is unable to convey the Spirit to anyone. Even if someone 'had devoured a hundred thousand Bibles,' he would only have a dead, 'written' faith. True faith is a spiritual experience: an experience of God's working in one's soul, which includes dreams and visions. Faith hears God speaking in the here and now, without mediation. The relationship of Word and faith, which, for Luther, is based on history and the Bible, becomes something internal for Müntzer, being pushed back to something purely subjective. Only those who hear God speaking to them in their own soul can understand and interpret the Scriptures correctly. And nobody can hear God without first having endured 'the cross and trials.'"[147] Wallmann continues: "Müntzer's mysticism of the cross does not remain passive; it releases powers that are fiercer, more impetuous and more immediate than the Reformation doctrine of the justification of faith, leading to more concrete action. Whereas Luther stays within the Augustinian-medieval tradition, expecting the end of the world and the Day of Judgment, Müntzer lives in the chiliastic hope of a kingdom of God on earth. Now is the time of the harvest, the time in which the chosen are separated from the godless. Müntzer sees himself as a prophet of the dawning kingdom. In fact, he sees himself as the chosen instrument through which God wants to work out the battle of the End Times." Müntzer ends up getting involved in the peasant revolt of the time (1525), is arrested during the Battle of Frankenhausen, and subsequently tortured and executed. He did not see the social motives of the peasant revolt.

This is a good place to make some more basic points about biblical prophecies regarding the second coming of Christ as a foundation for expecting a "millennial" reign (chiliasm). The starting point is the angel announcing after the ascension of Christ that he would come back the way he went (Luke 1:11). But the most significant texts are Revelation 1:7 and 20:1-6, particularly verses 4-6:

"He seized the dragon, the ancient serpent, which is the Devil or Satan, and tied it up for a thousand years and threw it into the abyss, which he locked over it and sealed, so that it could no longer lead the nations astray …" After that, it says: "Then I saw thrones; those who sat on them were entrusted with judgment. I also saw the souls of those who had been beheaded for their witness to Jesus and for the word of God, and who had not worshiped the beast or its image nor had accepted its mark on their foreheads or hands. They came to life and they reigned with Christ for a thousand years. The rest of the dead did not come to life until the thousand years were over. This is the first resurrection. Blessed and holy is the one who shares in the first resurrection. The second death has no power over these; they will be priests of God and of Christ, and they will reign with him for (the) thousand years."

That this only applies to the martyrs should not be taken too literally, since this is only a prophetic picture. What is meant are probably all those who suffered for their faith.

Paul, too, writes about the second coming of Christ, even before John wrote Revelation. And, like John, he does not refer to the judgment at the end of time but to the earlier resurrection of the believers. At first, he predicts this event for the near future, a time during which some of the believers would still be alive. Their mortal bodies would be changed into immortal bodies, he says. This makes clear that it is not only the martyrs who will experience the second coming of Christ. In First Corinthians 15:20-24, he writes, "But now Christ has been raised from the dead, the firstfruits of those who have fallen asleep. … but each one in proper order: Christ the firstfruits; then, at his coming, those who belong to Christ; then comes the end, when he hands over the kingdom to his God and Father, when he has destroyed every sovereignty and every authority and power." And then, in First Corinthians 15:51: "Behold, I tell you a mystery. We shall not all fall asleep, but we will all be changed." Furthermore, in First Thessalonians 4:15-17 he says, "Indeed, we tell you this, on the word of the Lord, that we who are alive, who are left until the coming of the Lord, will surely not precede those who have fallen asleep. … and the dead in Christ will rise first. Then we who are alive, who are left, will be caught up together with them in the clouds to meet the Lord in the air. Thus we shall always be with the Lord." In Second Thessalonians 2:1-12, Paul has changed his view on the timeframe of the event: "We ask you, brothers, with regard to the coming of our Lord Jesus Christ and our assembling with him, not to be shaken out of your minds suddenly, or to be alarmed either by a 'spirit,' or by an oral statement, or by a letter allegedly from us to the effect that the day of the Lord is at hand. Let no one deceive you in any way. For unless the apostasy comes first and the lawless one is revealed, the one doomed to perdition, who opposes and exalts himself above every so-called god and object of worship, so as to seat himself in the temple of God, claiming that he is a god—do you not recall that while I was still with you I told you these things? *And now you know what is restraining, that he may be revealed in his time.* For the mystery of lawlessness is already at work. But the one who restrains is to do so only for the present, until he is removed from the scene. And then the lawless one will be revealed, whom the Lord (Jesus) will kill with the breath of his mouth and render powerless by the manifestation of his coming." About the fate of the Jews, Paul writes in Romans 11:25f., "I do not want you to be unaware of this mystery, brothers, so that you will not become wise (in) your own estimation: a hardening has come upon Israel in part, until the full number of the Gentiles comes in, and thus all Israel will be saved, as it is written: 'The deliverer will come out of Zion, he will turn away godlessness from Jacob …'" (cf. **Luke 1:24**; Isa 59:20f; Hos 3:4f; **Zech 12:3 until the end**; Lk 21,25-28 etc.; Isa 51:17-23; Jer 25:15-26).

Of course, there were different speculations about what held back the man of lawlessness. The one that won the most adherents was that what held him back was the Roman Empire, which continued on in the West as the "Holy Roman Empire of the German Nation" and in the East as the czarist Russian empire. (The word *tsar* comes from *Caesar*, just like the German word for emperor, *Kaiser*.) The last emperor of the Holy Roman Empire of the German Nation resigned in 1806. He did this as a result of the French Revolution, which, incidentally, was completely atheistic. France did not belong to the empire. The Russian czardom ended in 1917, which opened up the field to atheistic communism. The second coming of Christ is preceded by a time of distress (cf. Mt 24:3-50; Mk 13; Lk 21:5-36).

In conclusion, we can say that the chiliasm of Müntzer had nothing to do with biblical prophecy. Long before him, similar misinterpretations caused Augustine to propagate a purely internal theory of chiliasm.[148]

B. The Baptist Movement[149]

Zwingli's Zurich was the place from which the Baptist movement began to spread. The Baptists split off from Zwingli's Protestantism (1523–1525) because he allowed the state to restrain his development. Adult baptism, also known as "believers' baptism," is the most well-known characteristic of the Baptists. This was probably also the main reason why the state condemned the movement. Someone who was not baptized was not a citizen of the state; such a person had no rights and no obligations. This was also one of the problems of the Jews who, because of that, received special protection from the emperor. For the Baptists, however, more important than citizenship was to try to "live separate from the world, in the form of free congregations modeled on the early apostolic congregations, closely adhering to the Bible and what it prescribes."[150] "They reject oaths and military service; no Baptist is supposed to hold a government office." "The Baptists are generally differentiated from the so-called Spiritualists, but the lines between them are blurred. It would not be wrong to call the entire movement that split off from the Reformation of the public church "spiritualistic": almost everywhere in this movement, the possession of the Spirit is being placed above the Word." The Baptists were driven completely underground.[151] According to Wallmann, this was equally true under Protestant authorities as well as under Catholic authorities, though this only applied to state authorities, not necessarily church authorities. The prince-archbishop of Basel, for instance, who had authority over what is today the region of Jura, permitted a group of Baptists to settle there after they had been expelled in 1706 from the canton of Bern by King Ludwig XIV. They still live there today, even though, during the Congress of Vienna in 1815, the prince-archbishop's part of Jura was allotted to the canton of Bern as compensation for the Vaud, which had separated from Bern and is still the canton of Vaud today. Finally, the primarily Catholic part of Jura the Vaud, which had been separated from the canton of Bern and became the independent canton of Jura.[152] The Baptists of the canton of Zurich hid in a cave, the "Baptist Cave" close to Bäretswil in the Zuercher Oberland. From there, they emigrated to the United States where they still live today. The Zuricher writer Gottfried Keller (1819–1890) wrote a novella called *Ursula* about the Baptists in the cave. Since he was the municipal writer of the town of Zurich, he had access to the state archive. However, the Baptists do not come off very well. In his depiction two of them try to get with force a closer relationship with Ursula. However she is able to resist. Baptism spread internationally (Swiss Brethren, Hutterites, Mennonites, Amish). Sometimes, it was combined with a completely unbiblical chiliasm, such as in Münster where Baptists managed to obtain a majority in local government. They decided to kill all the "godless." Community of goods and polygamy were introduced. The Bishop of Münster besieged the city, conquering it after fourteen months. This was the end of the Baptist rule there and did much to discredit the Baptist movement in general.

Chapter 4

Pietism[153]

A. Foundations

This movement of continental Protestantism arose in the seventeenth century after the Thirty Years' War and reached its heyday in the eighteenth century. There is a certain affinity to Jansenism and Quietism within the Catholic Church.[154]

The foundation is the work *True Christianity* in four volumes by Johann Arndt (1555–1621).[155] Instead of building on Luther, he draws on medieval (Catholic) mysticism: Johannes Tauler, *Theologica Germanica*, *Imitatio Christi*, the *Devotio Moderna*, the writings of the Franciscan Angela da Foigno.[156] He structures his ideas around the three ancient steps of mysticism—cleansing (*purgation*), enlightening (*illuminatio*), union of the soul with God (*unio mystica*)—and he speaks of self-denial, death of one's self-will, not clinging to the world, humility, serenity, tasting the sweetness of grace, and union of the soul with God.[157] He calls for a reorientation of religious life, away from an emphasis on pure doctrine, toward a greater emphasis on a pious life[158]—and also away from the Reformation doctrine on justification by faith, toward a piousness that emphasizes rebirth and sanctification, which is what Pietism is built on.[159]

I would like to add that I personally converted from Protestantism to Catholicism after reading Eckhart, Tauler and Suso. When I was fifteen, I thought about committing suicide because I saw no meaning in life, but then decided to simply become detached from life instead. I watched my life, as it were, from outside of myself, not really getting involved. Today, young people tend to seek escape in drugs and sex. On Easter when I was twenty-three, I became a believing Christian after a quote from G. W. F. Hegel's *Philosophy of History* had come to my mind: "World history moves to and from Jesus Christ."[160] I also received the gift of speaking in tongues, which freed me from the physical and psychological burden of my previous life, as I had grown up within the sect of Christian Science founded by M. B. Eddie where I had regularly attended Sunday school until I was twenty. More on that later.[161]

Back to the development of the Pietists. Besides asceticism and mysticism, there are also isolated pockets of charismata. A Pietist congregation in Herford, for instance, experienced their own Pentecost. "After a communal love-feast, a kind of ecstasy came over the assembly, a 'Christian shouting, jumping, dancing and kissing.' The members of the congregation gave up their monastic asceticism, married among each other and—for the sake of the preservation and multiplication of God's Kingdom—produced children who were supposedly born without sin."[162] It is clear that, in this case, a work of the Spirit was soon pervaded by an evil spirit.

An influential figure within Pietism was Gerhard Tersteegen (1697–1769),[163] known today (next to Paul Gerhardt) primarily through his songs. On Maundy Thursday of 1724, he used his own blood to declare in writing that he belonged completely to the Savior: "My Jesus! I commit myself to you, my savior and bridegroom, Jesus Christ, as your eternal possession, without any reservation." He later repeated this declaration on several occasions. He did it at the end of a period of years marked by spiritual drought and darkness, after which he once more experienced the light of the divine grace. He called it his "second conversion."[164]

Central to his thought is "godliness," by which he understood a piousness from the heart that was given directly by God, opposed to all the outward, formulaic and moralistic Christianity of the institutional church.[165] His verse lyric of the "wayfaring man" takes inspiration from Angelus Silesus, a convert to Catholicism.[166] He also published what he called *Select Biographies of Holy Souls*, a biographical collection in three volumes, depicting twenty-five Catholic men and women, primarily from the time of the Counter Reformation, who belonged to different orders, including that of the Jesuits, and who were characterized by their solitary, anti-worldly lifestyle and mystical-quietist experience of God.[167] He thought that there were more truly evangelical Christians in the Catholic Church than in the Protestant churches.[168] Tersteegen remained unmarried. On behalf of a friend who founded a community with seven like-minded friends, he wrote what basically amounted to a Pietist monastic rule.[169]

Pietism within the Lutheran Church has its true beginning in 1670 with the founding of the "Collegium pietatis" and, in 1675, with the publication of the Pietist manifesto *Pia Desidaria* by Philipp Jakob Spener.[170] Spener is called the "Father of Pietism," but another father of Pietism is Johann Jakob Schütz,[171] who was especially influenced by the medieval mystic Johannes Tauler[172] and who founded a Pietism that separated itself from the church.

Though Spener supported the orthodox teaching of the baptismal rebirth (of the baptized infants), he believed that most Christians had not experienced this rebirth. In his view, they had fallen from the grace of baptism and needed to be born again. This is not too different from today's Catholic notion of the renewal of baptism that is celebrated collectively for the whole congregation every Easter mass. Spener emphasizes the general priesthood as a spiritual priesthood. All believers are "ministers," he says; there are no laypersons.[173] Theology students should read Johannes Tauler, *Theologia Germanica*, Thomas à Kempis.[174] Finally, in opposition to Luther, Spener also became open again to a future-oriented chiliasm.[175] He successfully defended his teaching that true theology cannot exist without enlightenment through the Holy Spirit.[176]

Spener had a hard-working student, August Hermann Francke (1663–1727), who managed to transcend Lutheran orthodoxy and establish an ideological power that had a forming influence on the Protestant church (Hallish Pietism).[177]

In 1687, Francke started to have doubts whether he actually had faith, filling him with an "inner misery."[178] One Sunday night before he went to bed, he sank on his knees, pleading with God in great fear to save him from his "miserable condition." His prayer was answered instantly. Suddenly, he was overcome by a deep assurance. Francke felt born again and experienced the truth of what Luther had written in his *Preface to*

Romans: "Faith is a work of God in us, which changes us and brings us to birth anew from God." Francke writes in his autobiography that from then on it was easy for him to deny the world and live solely for God. This became typical for the later Pietist conversion experience, which was something still unknown to the likes of Arndt and Spener. Both of these stood in the tradition of Luther's teaching that uncertainty and doubt were part of the experience of faith and had to be endured as divine trials (*simul iustus et peccator*). Now, with the new development, there was also a new interpretation of Romans 7:14-25. In addition to Francke, another shaping influence on Hallish Pietism was Calvinist-Reformed teaching.[179]

There was also a wave of ecstatic spiritual experiences in Middle Germany, with which Francke had connections.[180] Women, often simple maids, had visions and heard voices.[181] In Halberstadt, two women predicted the imminent downfall of both church and state. In Quedlingburg, there was a woman who sweated blood, and in Erfurt someone sang verses about the soon-to-come return of the Lord. Francke showed solidarity with theses prophetesses, saying that God was "proclaiming his miracles through such things," which would "burst forth even more gloriously in the future." Among radical Pietists, there were whole congregations that experienced their own Pentecost.[182] These were the so-called "Inspired" who had convulsions and trance-like experiences during which they received "orations" that others wrote down and distributed as divine revelations.[183] In 1728, Johann Friedrich Rock (1678–1749) became the leader of the "true inspirational congregations," serving as a spiritual supervisor through frequent travels. Count Zinzendorf spoke highly of him for many years, recognizing him as a pious man in whom there was no wrong. Later, however, there was a rupture between the two. The last flourishing of the inspirational congregations came in the nineteenth century. Starting in 1842, about a thousand Inspired emigrated to North America and founded the Amana Church Society (named after Song of Solomon 4:8) in Iowa, of which some remainders can still be found today.[184]

Finally, we should mention the Moravian Church of Herrnhut, led by Count Nikolaus Ludwig von Zinzendorf (1700–1760).[185] The movement saw itself as "interdenominational,"[186] and Zinzendorf had friendly relations even with the archbishop of Paris, Cardinal Louis-Antoine de Noailles (1651–1729) and published a booklet with songs and prayers for Catholics.[187] While celebrating Communion one day in 1727, the Moravians had an overwhelming communal experience that led the Herrnhuters, who had been divided up to this point, to embrace each other in heartfelt love. In retrospect, they saw this experience as a "new Pentecost."[188] As mentioned above, Zinzendorf's contact with the Inspirational Churches came to an end (after six years). The reason for this was that Zinzendorf moved away from Pietism, turning to Lutheranism instead. With John Wesley (1703–1791), too, there was a falling-out after Wesley's conversion experience, which had been influenced by the Herrnhuters. In spite of evangelisms conducted jointly by the Moravians and Methodist Anglicans who came from Wesley, there were irreconcilable differences about questions of holiness and the Law (1741).[189]

B. Radical Pietism[190]

One of the main marks of radical Pietism was that it separated itself completely from what its adherents perceived as the incurably depraved and unreformable (Reformed/Lutheran) church. Not only did these Pietists distance themselves from the church, some of them also distanced themselves from the world—by renouncing marriage, for instance.[191] To this end, Tauler served as a model. There was also a truly biblical chiliastic expectation of the future.[192] In 1683, they founded Germantown in Philadelphia, Pennsylvania, the first German settlement in North America.[193]

C. Evaluating Pietism

Wallmann calls Pietism a deeply Protestant phenomenon. Pietism, he says, deepened the divide between the Protestant denominations and Roman Catholicism.[194] This is not at all how I view the matter. As we have seen, Pietism re-assimilated teachings that were clearly Catholic, especially in its spirituality. Wallmann, however, refers to two specific points, namely the chiliastic expectation of the future and, connected with it, the expected fall of papal Rome. In answer, it can be said that neither the Catholic nor the Orthodox Church ever condemned true chiliasm. Augustine only condemned a clearly false chiliasm and, in reaction to its errors, applied the relevant prophecies in the Bible to our spiritual life in the here and now. Of course, these prophecies may well be relevant for now, but that does not preclude truly prophetic chiliasm—a fact which Augustine did not deny. The following passage from his *De Civitate Dei* shows this quite clearly: "The evangelist John has spoken of these two resurrections in the book which is called the Apocalypse, but in such a way that some Christians do not understand the first of the two, and so construe the passage into ridiculous fancies. For the Apostle John says in the foresaid book, 'And I saw an angel come down from heaven. … Blessed and holy is he that hath part in the first resurrection: on such the second death hath no power; but they shall be priests of God and of Christ, and shall reign with Him a thousand years.' Those who, on the strength of this passage, have suspected that the first resurrection is future and bodily, have been moved, among other things, specially by the number of a thousand years, as if it were a fit thing that the saints should thus enjoy a kind of Sabbath-rest during that period, a holy leisure after the labors of the six thousand years since man was created, and was on account of his great sin dismissed from the blessedness of paradise into the woes of this mortal life, so that thus, as it is written, 'One day is with the Lord as a thousand years, and a thousand years as one day,' (2Pe 3:8) there should follow on the completion of six thousand years, as of six days, a kind of seventh-day Sabbath in the succeeding thousand years; and that it is for this purpose the saints rise, viz. to celebrate this Sabbath. And this opinion would not be objectionable, if it were believed that the joys of the saints in that Sabbath shall be spiritual, and consequent on the presence of God; for I myself, too, once held this opinion. But, as they assert that those who then rise again shall enjoy the leisure of immoderate carnal banquets, furnished with an amount of meat and drink such as not only to shock the feeling of the temperate, but even to surpass the measure of credulity itself, such assertions can be believed only by the carnal. They who do believe them are called by the spiritual Chiliasts, which we may literally reproduce by the name Millenarians. It were a tedious process to refute these opinions point by point: we prefer proceeding to show how that passage of Scripture should be understood."[195] Following this, Augustine explains that the Millennium has already begun with the Christians now living and spells out what significance this has for them. The fact that the Catholic Church followed this teaching in practice does not preclude the possibility of a future Millennium in line with biblical prophecy. The official statement of the Catholic Church on this issue is as follows (Decree of the Holy Office, July 19/21, 1944): "In recent times on several occasions this Supreme Sacred Congregation of the Holy Office has been asked what must be thought of the system of mitigated Millenarianism, which teaches, for example, that Christ the Lord before the final judgment, whether or not preceded by the resurrection of the many just, will come visibly to rule over this world. The answer is [as confirmed by the pope on June 20, 1944]: The system of mitigated Millenarianism cannot be taught safely."[196] A "mitigated Millenarianism" is in line with what Augustine originally advocated. Of course, the Church has always rejected a this-worldly chiliasm in the vein of Münster etc.

Besides, the question whether the Roman papacy will come to an end when Christ returns is hardly ever discussed in Catholic circles. The fact is that the papacy changed significantly in 1870. The Italian Risorgimento conquered the States of the Church, thus bringing its worldly power to an end. This did not change significantly even when Mussolini later founded the state of the Vatican. On the other hand, the spiritual significance of the pope increased when it was decided during the First Vatican Council that the pope was infallible in certain respects.

As a final point, it should be mentioned that Pietists shifted away from the Reformation doctrine of justification by faith toward a piousness based on rebirth and sanctification, which was the foundation on which they built.[197] Paul's declaration "I live, no longer I, but Christ lives in me"[198] became central, in line with Jesus' statement "I am the way, the truth, and the life."[199] What makes Pietists non-Catholic is their rejection of the Catholic view on apostolicity. Thus, they are precursors of the end of the Catholic age, as represented by the woman in the wilderness.

Chapter 5

Developments within the Catholic Church

A. Pope Leo XIII's Consecration of the World to the Holy Spirit on January 1, 1901

In the beginning of his papacy, Pope John XXIII beatified Elena Guerra (1958–1963), calling her a "missionary of the veneration of the Holy Spirit in our time."[200] The fact is that, through Elena Guerra, something was set into motion that was of great church-historical significance, having been predicted by Joachim of Fiore as the "age of the Spirit."

Elena Guerra, born in Lucca in Tuscany, was the daughter of deeply religious, aristocratic parents, Antonio Guerra and Faustina Franceschi. She was born when her mother fell from a carriage, and throughout her childhood and youth she was sickly. At the same time, she had a spiritual drive from an early age. She would have liked to have received a more advanced education, which was denied her. Secretly, she learned Latin and read books, especially the Bible (in Latin). She also had missionary fervor. Though bedridden between the ages of twenty-two and twenty-seven, she published brochures during this time and founded a community for women called the "Spiritual Friends," starting with five people but growing later to five hundred.

After her recovery in 1894, she joined a group of "ladies of charity" as well as the Association of the Daughters of Mary of St. Agnes where she later became chairwoman. She said that one reason she joined these groups was to gain more independence from home. Together with her father, she visited the First Vatican Council in Rome in 1870, which gave her spiritual inspiration. On one anniversary of her baptism she gave her life to Jesus Christ. She also reported having received a "flood of graces" in 1870-71, after which she founded the community of the "Worshippers of Jesus in the Sacrament of the Altar" (of the transubstantiated Communion bread). This, however, turned out not to be her path, she felt, and she experienced a season of spiritual dryness. Next, toward the end of 1872, she founded a secular institute in Lucca that ran a girl's school. What was essential for her was that the women who were involved there were not locked up in a convent but could move about freely, that is, they were oblates. In 1882, she was able to purchase her own house and spent one month in uninterrupted Eucharistic worship (worship of the transubstantiated Communion bread), praying "Come, Creator Spirit."[201] Later, she felt led to bring people into a close relationship with the Holy Spirit.[202] She writes in her diary on her baptismal day: "After being reborn in water, one also has to be reborn in the Holy Spirit." "Those who are born also have to grow." The fact is that, even as a child, she had a very close relationship with the Holy Spirit. She writes: "The veneration of the Holy Spirit is something that has always burned in my heart, even though nobody recommended this to me and I did not read anything that might have taught me to love it." "Even as a little child, I felt like being in heaven when I was in church for Pentecost novena [the nine days between the Ascension and Pentecost]. I always felt a great sadness that this, the most important of all devotions [...] has been almost entirely forgotten now." At the time, the Holy Spirit was not a topic of any importance among Catholics at large, and the world was in a sorry spiritual state in the nineteenth century. Elena initiated prayers that centered around the Holy Spirit, and she contacted many priests and bishops. Nothing much came of it until she had the idea in 1886 to write directly to the pope and ask him to make her concern known. She wanted there to be groups around the world that constantly prayed like the disciples of Jesus prayed together with Mary and the other women after the Ascension. At first, others advised her against writing to the pope. Then, however, in 1893, a kitchen worker in the convent (Sister Erminia Giorgetti) told her that the Lord said she should write a letter to the pope. She said that the Lord told her, "I want you to say to the Mother (Elena) she should call back all believers through the *New Upper Room* to *a universal prayer to my heart. ...* Tell her that she should write a letter to the Holy Father, asking him to call believers to a perpetual prayer. They should pray much to the Holy Spirit and, by doing so, try to call all hearts back to God."

Even though her spiritual counselor accepted Erminia's words as authentic, Elena still hesitated a while to follow Jesus' commission. On March 27, 1894, then, she gathered the courage to have her spiritual counselor deliver her booklet *The New Upper Room* to the pope.

On April 17, 1895, Elena finally overcame her reticence and wrote a petition to the pope.[203] She asked him to order all parishes to keep the Pentecost novena between Ascension and Pentecost, the same way the Apostles did together with Mary and the other women.[204] She wrote, "There are many novenae that are being prayed, and this is good, but the novena that was prayed at the order of the Savior himself and was kept by Mary and the Apostles has now largely fallen into oblivion." And then she adds, "Oh if only there would be unified and ardent prayers sent to heaven from all sides of Christendom, as of old in the upper room in Jerusalem, to plead with the Spirit of God. How much blessing and grace such petition would bring!"[205] Finally, she refers to her booklet that she enclosed, *The New Upper Room*, which suggests a novena to the Holy Spirit.[206] This novena to the Holy Spirit[207] asks specifically for the gifts of the Spirit rather than just for his general visitation. Every prayer for the day ends with the verse from Psalms: "Lord, send forth your Spirit, and the face of the earth will be renewed" (Ps 104:30).[208] However, the New American Bible, which is the only translation approved for use at mass in the dioceses of the United States, translates Psalm 104, verses 27-30 as follows: "All of these (your creatures) look to you to give them food in due time. When you give it to them, they gather; when you open your hand, they are well filled. When you hide your face, they panic. Take away their breath, they perish and return to the dust. Send forth your spirit, they are created and you renew the face of the earth." This means the verse is not actually a petition for the Holy Spirit.

Elena Guerra also alleges that Jesus Christ commanded the Apostles to go the upper room to pray for the Holy Spirit. Actually, though, that is not what it says in the Holy Scriptures. Jesus only commanded the Apostles to stay in Jerusalem where they would be baptized with the Holy Spirit (Acts 1:4f. & 8 / Lk 24:49). It was their own idea to gather with Mary and the women in the upper room. There they prayed, but it does not say about what (Acts 1:13). Jesus Christ said clearly that he (or the Father) would send the Spirit, and what comes across in this is that those who have not already received the Spirit also cannot pray for the Spirit. Jesus had already breathed on the Apostles and, through his breath, given them the Spirit (John 20:22), and Mary received the Lord through the Spirit (Mt 1:18; Lk 1:35). Regarding the other women and the brothers of Jesus, however, it is not clear whether they received the Spirit before. Also, there were an additional 120 disciples present (Acts 1:15).

Of course, at the time of Elena Guerra, the situation was different. The Spirit had already been poured out, and those who had the Spirit could ask for a deeper experience of the Spirit. As it says: those who have will be given more (Mt 13:12; 25:29; Mk 4:25; Lk 8:18; 19:16). However, it is emphasized that almost no one at the time was open to the Spirit anymore.[209]

Fourteen days after receiving Elena Guerra's letter, the pope issued the breve *Provida Matris Charitate* (on May 5, 1895).[210] This breve was not exclusively addressed to the bishops but to all believers.[211] In it, the pope says that Christians are "united in faith in the Spirit, united in the piousness in works," and he expresses his wish that Catholics unite with him in prayer. To this end, no time seems to be more appropriate than the time after the Ascension when the Apostles gathered to persist in prayer, together with Mary, the Mother of Jesus, waiting for the promised power from on high and the gifts of the Spirit.[212] He also recommends that believers keep saying the prayer, "Send forth your spirit, they [your creatures] are created and you renew the face of the earth"[213] Through the unanimity of this prayer, a great hope would rise among Catholics that this would "lead to the reconciliation of the separated brothers and sisters … for they too have a mind that is in accordance with the teachings of Jesus Christ (Phil 2:5) and will one day join us in the same faith and hope, being enclosed by the sweet bond of perfect love."[214]

After this breve, Elena Guerra wrote four more letters to the pope, driven, as she was, by her "sister in the faith" Erminia who again received what she believed were divine inspirations. The main goal of the letters was to advocate an even greater devotion to the Holy Spirit and turn the Pentecost novena into a perpetual prayer in the Church at large.[215] She saw this as a way to awaken many Christians who had become lukewarm, as well as to save many who were lost. She makes particular reference to the evil spiritual influence of the Free Masons.[216]

It is a fact that, after the end of the Holy Roman Empire, the nineteenth century became the birthplace of many evil spirits—not only the influence of atheism in the French Revolution but also the *Manifesto* of Karl Marx in 1848, the psychology of Freud and C.G. Jung and a more intense growth of esotericism through Steiner and others, not to forget the anti-Catholicism in Germany and the conquest of the States of the Church in Italy.

After Elena Guerra's fourth letter, on Pentecost of May 9, 1887, the pope issued a circular letter about the Holy Spirit, his encyclical *Divinum illud munus*.[217] After this, Elena Guerra wrote five additional letters. In the fifth, dated October 15, 1900, she asked the pope whether the new year could be started with the prayer *Veni Spiritus Creator*,[218] to be sung at the beginning of midnight mass or in every church on the first mass of the year. On January 1, 1901, the pope did sing this hymn. He was already ninety years old, and I think others joined him in the singing.[219] I do not know if this happened before a mass or on the balcony of St. Peter's Square. The following is the official English translation of the Latin text.[220]

Come, Holy Ghost, Creator, come
from thy bright heav'nly throne;
come, take possession of our souls,
and make them all thine own.

Thou who art called the Paraclete,
best gift of God above,
the living spring, the living fire,

sweet unction and true love.

Thou who art sevenfold in thy grace,
finger of God's right hand;
his promise, teaching little ones
to speak and understand.

O guide our minds with thy blest light,
with love our hearts inflame;
and with thy strength, which ne'er decays,
confirm our mortal frame.

Far from us drive our deadly foe;
true peace unto us bring;
and through all perils lead us safe
beneath thy sacred wing.

Through thee may we the Father know,
through thee th'eternal Son
and thee the Spirit of them both,
thrice-blessed three in One.

The original Latin version was most likely written by Rhabanus Maurus, abbot of Fulda and archbishop of Mainz, who lived at the end of the eighth and in the first half of the ninth century. The text quickly gained a popular place in the liturgy and was translated by Luther, Terstegen, and Angelus Silesius—and later by Goethe—in German.[221]

Soon after January 1, 1901, the pope fell ill and died in 1903. There are still some things that remain to be said about Pope Leo XIII, though.

B. More about Pope Leo XIII

1. General Remarks[222]

Vincenzo Gioacchino Pecci (1810–1903) became Pope in 1878. Being already sixty-eight, which was a great age at the time, he was expected to be merely a "transitional" pope. Yet he reached an age of nine-three and published eighty-six encyclicals. His most well-known was the encyclical *Rerum novarum* in 1891, through which he founded the Catholic social teaching for the industrial age. Another important encyclical was the *Providentissimus Deus*, making the Holy Scriptures more accessible to Catholics after the restrictions that had followed the Reformation. In view of the growing globalization, he also started a reform of church structures after the Papal State had come to an end in 1871 through the Italian Risorgimento. As far as he was concerned, however, he thought his most important contribution was the encyclical *Annum sacrum* in 1899, about the veneration of the sacred heart of Jesus.[223] His testament is generally seen to be the encyclical *Mirae caritatis* in 1902, about the Eucharist.[224]

2. Consecrating the World to the Heart of Jesus

On June 11, 1899, Pope Leo XIII consecrated the world to the Heart of Jesus, which he announced and explained in his encyclical *Annum sacrum* on May 25, 1899.[225] His initiative came after his 1897 encyclical *Divinum illud munus* about the Holy Spirit,[226] but before his consecration of the world to the Holy Spirit on January 1, 1901, both of which happened as a result of letters by Elena Guerra. The consecration to the heart of Jesus, too, came as a direct result of a petition, this one by a sister of the "Order of Our Dear Woman of the Love of the Good Shepherd," Mary of the Divine Heart, born Mary Droste zu Vischering (in the area of Münster in Westphalia, Germany), who, at the time, was Mother Superior of a house in Porto, Portugal.

There is a spiritual connection between the devotion to the Sacred Heart of Jesus and the consecration to the Holy Spirit. In order to make this connection clear, we first have to discuss what the Sacred Heart of Jesus is about, which has a long history, going back to the presence of Jesus himself.[227]

The foundation for this teaching was the Council of Ephesus (A.D. 431), which said that Jesus Christ had two natures: the divine nature as Son of God the Father, and the created nature as the son of Mary through the Holy Spirit. The two natures are joined in the "hypotastic union," meaning there is only one person. Later the natures are also called "substance" or "essence." The Jesus you can see, hear, and feel is not his essential quality but only his accidental quality. Applying this to the devotion to the Sacred Heart of Jesus: it relates to the one person of the two natures, not to the human (created) heart of Jesus. This heart was not pierced during his lifetime and it was not it that suffered but the person who suffered—because of the sinfulness of humanity. It is this person who encompasses the divinity of Christ who, more than anything, loves us.

The person who initiated essentially the devotion to the Sacred Heart of Jesus was Sister Margarete-Marie Alacoque of Paray-le-Monial in Burgundy.[228] She had repeatedly appearances and words of Jesus Christ, which she wrote down be the order of her spiritual leader.[228] First I would like to mention, that the Lord commissioned Margarete Alacoque to make an image of Him with a symbolic heart on a chest with a cross, crown of thorns, and flame of fire.[229]

This image was to be put up in people's houses, to edify believers. Obviously, the heart was only symbolic, as it was not meant to be the human heart of Jesus. What was most essential are the cross and the crown of thorns, both of which Jesus had to suffer as a human. And the flame of fire is a reference to his divine nature, which takes part in the suffering.

However, the main locution of Jesus was this:[230] "Behold the gown of innocence with which I envelop your soul so that, from now on, you only live a divinized life, that is, to live in such a way that it is not you who live but I who live in you. For I am your life and you should only live in and through me. I want you to act in such a way as if you did not act, instead letting me act in and through you, and that you cast all your cares on me. You can no longer have any will of your own, instead letting me do through you what I want, in all things and all places."

Pope Pius XII teaches in his 1956 encyclical *Haurietis aquas,*[231] par. 21: "His Heart, the noblest part of human nature, is hypostatically united to the Person of the divine Word. Consequently, there must be paid to it that worship of adoration with which the Church honors the Person of the

Incarnate Son of God Himself."[232] Compare par. 81, according to which the gift of the Love of Christ is the Holy Spirit. Also, par. 85: "Nothing therefore prevents our adoring the Sacred Heart of Jesus Christ as having a part in and being the natural and expressive symbol of the abiding love with which the divine Redeemer is still on fire for mankind. Though it is no longer subject to the varying emotions of this mortal life, yet it lives and beats and is united inseparably with the Person of the divine Word and, in Him and through Him, with the divine Will. Since then the Heart of Christ is overflowing with love both human and divine and rich with the treasure of all graces which our Redeemer acquired by His life, sufferings and death, it is therefore the enduring source of that charity which His Spirit pours forth on all the members of His Mystical Body."

This is followed by par. 86: "And so the Heart of our Savior reflects in some way the image of the divine Person of the Word and, at the same time, of His twofold nature, the human and the divine; in it we can consider not only the symbol but, in a sense, the summary of the whole mystery of our redemption. When we adore the Sacred Heart of Jesus Christ, we adore in it and through it both the uncreated love of the divine Word and also its human love and its other emotions and virtues …"

It is a fact that the devotion to the Sacred Heart of Jesus has a close affinity to the Catholic Eucharist, in which the body of Christ, changed into bread, is worshipped. This affinity is something to which Mary of the Divine Heart already testified in her youth: "I was never able to separate the devotion to the Sacred Heart of Jesus from the most sacred of altar sacraments, and never will I be able to explain how many graces the most sacred heart of Jesus granted me through the most sacred altar sacrament."[233] It is important to mention that, starting in 1873, the castle chapel of her parents in Darfeld celebrated the Sacred Heart of Jesus on Fridays by suspending the Blessed Sacrament on those days.[234] However, one should keep in mind that, at the time, laypeople in the Catholic Church rarely took Communion.

At this point it needs to be explained what, according to Catholic doctrine, is expected from Holy Communion. When Jesus says on the Thursday before his crucifixion of the bread, "This is my body," and of the wine, "This is my blood," then this is exactly what happens.

However, this change only affects the substance, the being, not the material appearance that we can perceive with our senses. And the most essential part of this being is the hypostatic union with the Divinity of Christ. That is why Lutherans, who have a similar concept, do not speak of transubstantiation but of consubstantiation. The disciples did not taste this process with their tongues but, in a manner of speaking, with their hearts. One can compare this with the disciples on the road to Emmaus who met the risen Lord without recognizing him, but who later said, "Were not our hearts burning (within us)?"[235] Now, when Jesus says, "Do this in remembrance of me," he does not just mean the eating of bread and the drinking of wine but rather their transformation into his body and his blood. Today, the one presiding over Holy Communion says in the name of Christ, "This is my body and blood," and he does so by the Holy Spirit and with the authority of Christ. To modern sensibilities, the speaking with the authority of someone else might seem a little strange, but we should realize that judicial authorization is a modern invention, unknown to Roman law, which had trusteeships instead.[236] From all this, it becomes clear that the worship of the changed bread is related to the devotion to the Sacred Heart of Jesus.

Finally, it should be mentioned that both the devotion of the Sacred Heart of Jesus and the Eucharistic worship were connected to an act of giving one's life to Christ. To show this, I cite Pope Leo XIII who wrote in his encyclical *Annun sacrum* on May 25, 1899:

"And since there is in the Sacred Heart a symbol and a sensible image of the infinite love of Jesus Christ which moves us to love one another, therefore is it fit and proper that we should consecrate ourselves to His most Sacred Heart—an act which is nothing else than an offering and a binding of oneself to Jesus Christ, seeing that whatever honor, veneration and love is given to this divine Heart is really and truly given to Christ Himself."

And the pope's suggested formulation of declaring one's consecration was as follows:

"Most sweet Jesus, redeemer of the human race, look down upon us, humbly prostrate before your altar. We are yours and yours we wish to be; but to be more surely united with you, behold each one of us freely consecrates himself today to your most sacred heart. Many, indeed, have never known you, many too, despising your precepts, have rejected you. Have mercy on them all, most merciful Jesus, and draw them to your sacred heart. Be you king, O Lord, not only of the faithful who have never forsaken you, but also of the prodigal children who have abandoned you; grant that they may quickly return to their father's house, lest they die of wretchedness and hunger. Be you king of those who are deceived by erroneous opinions, or whom discord keeps aloof, and call them back to the harbor of truth and unity of faith, so that soon there may be but one flock and one shepherd. Be you king also of all those who sit in the ancient superstition of the Gentiles, and refuse not you to deliver them out of darkness into the light and kingdom of God. Grant, O Lord, to your Church, assurance of freedom and immunity from harm; give peace and order to all nations, and make the earth resound from pole to pole with one cry: Praise to the divine heart that wrought our salvation; to it be glory and honor forever."[237]

This also makes clear that both the consecration to the Heart of Jesus as well as the Eucharistic worship have something to do with the Baptism with the Holy Spirit. The basis for Spirit baptism is more than just faith and water baptism. Though it is true that faith and water baptism also transmit the Spirit, there is still a difference. In addition, Catholics have the element of Confirmation. There are Pentecostals who differentiate between the Spirit that we have and the Spirit that has us.[238] Either way, the Pentecostal view is that Baptism with the Spirit is preconditioned on prayer, obedience, and submission to God.[239] Since this submission to God, giving one's life to Jesus Christ, is such an essential element, I take the view that devotion to the Sacred Heart of Jesus is closely connected to the consecration to the Holy Spirit and that Pope Leo XIII was right to put the two closely together. On a more personal note, I can say that when I (audibly) pray in tongues, I have a similar feeling in my heart as during the Eucharist, and someone else has told me that they were moved in their heart when they heard me pray in tongues in a Pentecostal congregation.

C. The History of the Devotion to the Sacred Heart of Jesus

The devotion to the Sacred Heart of Jesus can already be found in the Holy Scriptures, most markedly in the Gospel of the Apostle John when he describes the meal before Passover.[240] There, he calls himself the disciple "whom Jesus loved." He lay by Jesus' side. In order to ask Jesus who would betray him, he "leaned back against Jesus' chest" and asked him, "Master, who is it?"[241] John does not mention that it was during this meal that Jesus changed the bread into his body and the wine into his blood. This is possibly meant to show that John's relationship to the Heart of Jesus was, in a way, equal to Holy Communion. It is John who tells us that Jesus already talked at an earlier point about eating his flesh and drinking his blood. The Last Supper had been on his heart for a long time, since he said that he was the bread that his Father sent down from heaven.[242] He was the bread of life, and those who came to him would never go hungry again. He continued: "Whoever eats my flesh and drinks my blood has eternal life, and I will raise him on the last day. For my flesh is true food, and my blood is true drink. Whoever eats my flesh and drinks my blood remains in me and I in him. Just as the living Father sent me and I have life because of the Father, so also the one who feeds on me will have life because of me. This is the bread that came down from heaven. Unlike your ancestors who ate (the manna) and still died, whoever eats this bread will live forever."[243]

However, Jesus followed these statements by saying, "It is the spirit that gives life, while the flesh is of no avail. The words I have spoken to you are spirit and life."[244] What he meant, I think, was that it was the Divinity behind the flesh and the blood that works the effect.

While he spoke those words, Jesus already thought about the Last Supper on the day before his death. Luke testifies that Jesus said, "I have eagerly desired to eat this Passover with you before I suffer."[245]

What Jesus says about Communion is also largely true of the devotion to the Sacred Heart of Jesus. In both cases, what is important is that we are in Jesus and Jesus is in us. This is repeated several times in the Holy Scriptures.[246] This is the *perichoresis* or *intercession* that is also said of the three Persons of God. In the Old Testament it speaks of seeing God face to face, better translated as "eye to eye." That is, the person seeing

God does not see whether his eyes are brown or blue. Rather, he sees intuitively what God thinks about him and desires from him.[247] In the relationship between us and Christ, we can say that he is the head and we are the body.

This close connection with Jesus Christ also means that, through our faith in him, we die with him and rise as new creatures. Hence, Paul can say of himself, "I live, no longer I, but Christ lives in me."[248] This is the faith that reveals to us a mystery, called the *mysterion tou pistou* in ancient Greek, which Hieronymus translated as *sacramentum* in Latin. Unfortunately, the modern English word *mystery* does not quite have the same connotation today. What is meant is not that someone believes something that he will never understand but that his faith is an experience that is inaccessible for unbelievers. That is why the French translate it as *mystère de la foie* and not as *secret de la foie*, even though they usually eliminate all foreign words. It is a mystery in the sense of mysticism, which cannot be translated and which goes back to Paganism.[249]

In the Gospels, there is an occurrence that closely resembles this kind of faith and can be seen as a precursor to the devotion to the Sacred Heart of Jesus: the anointing of Jesus with the nard oil from the alabaster jar. It was the event of which Jesus said that it would be mentioned wherever the Gospel was going to be preached.[250] Or, to put it more accurately: it is mentioned wherever the Gospel is *truly* preached, that is, in all its depth. My book *Das Nardenöl aus dem Alabastergefäss; Von Tod und Auferstehung Christi ergriffen wie Maria* ("The Nard Oil and the Alabaster Jar: Moved Like Mary by the Death and Resurrection of Christ")[251] looks in detail at this dimension of the faith, and several chapters deal with the devotion to the Sacred Heart of Jesus.[252] For how the devotion to the Sacred Heart of Jesus developed from its beginnings in the Gospels, I refer the reader to this book. Here, I will limit myself to quoting what Gertrude the Great of Helfta (1256–1302) wrote in her diary-like work *The Herald of Divine Love:*

"While she (Gertrude), at the Matins of the feast of the same Apostle (John), prayed in her usual devout fashion, there was present with her the disciple whom Jesus loved, which love makes it right that all those who love should love him as well, and the disciple spoke to her in a most kindly way. … He answered, 'Come with me, chosen of my heart. Let us rest on the breast of the Lord, which flows with sweetness and contains all the treasures of blessedness.' … The movement of the most sacred pulsations from which the divine Heart was quickened without end caused her indescribable delight, and she said to Saint John, 'Have not you also, beloved of God, felt the delight of the most sacred pulsations when you rested at the Last Supper against this same breast whose joys now move me so?' He answered, 'Yes, I felt the truth …' To this, she said, 'Why did you keep it secret and did not write anything of it down for our benefit?' He answered, 'It was my task to write down a word from the uncreated Word of God for the benefit of the church, which was still young, a word that the understanding of all of humanity could grapple with until the end of the world without ever fully comprehending it. The language of the blissful pulsations is kept for these later times, to warm, by hearing such mysteries, a world that is growing old and cold in God's love.'"[253]

In his encyclical *Harieis aquas*,[254] Pope Pius XII mentions not only Gertrude of Helfta as a medieval witness of the devotion to the Sacred Heart of Jesus but also Bonaventura, Albert the Great, Catherine of Siena, Heinrich Suo, Peter Canisius, and Francis de Sales. After medieval times, we should mention John Eudes and—absolutely essential—Margarite-Marie Alacoque (1647–1690) who received inspirations from the Lord, thus giving the devotion to the Sacred Heart of Jesus new impetus. After her death, this new religiosity seemed to spread fast. However, she was opposed by Jansenism and, later, the atheism of the French Revolution. Still, the Sacred Congregation of Rites, Pope Clemens XIII, the bishops of Poland, and the so-called "Roman Archfraternity of the Sacred Heart of Jesus" permitted the liturgical feast of 1765. But it was only in 1856 that Pope Pius IX, at the request of the bishops in France and almost the entire Catholic world, extended the Feast of the Most Sacred Heart of Jesus to the entire Church and established it as a regular celebration.[255] On the occasion of the First Vatican Council (1869–1870), the majority of bishops made the proposal to raise the feast to the highest possible status, asking the pope to consecrate the entire Church to the Sacred Heart of Jesus. This idea, however, was never implemented, since troops of the Italian

Risorgimento occupied Rome, causing the premature dissolution of the Council in 1870. In 1875, P. Henri Ramière S. J. handed in a petition signed by 525 bishops, asking the people to consecrate "Rome and the whole earth" to the Heart of Jesus. The pope did not want to make a decision but responded to the bishops by having a prayer of consecration written. He died in 1878, and the matter seemed to come to rest.[256]

Finally, God brought Sister Mary of the Divine Heart, countess of Droste zu Vischering (1863–1899), to suggest to the people to consecrate the whole of humanity to the Sacred Heart of Jesus,[257] as already mentioned.

What I want to stress here is that the devotion to the Sacred Heart of Jesus is an act of faith, arising from the heart under the influence of Christ and the Holy Spirit, who conveys the experience of the death and resurrection of Christ in a completely different way than the intellectual creed that is said at baptism and at the renewal of baptism on Easter.

Chapter 6

Pentecostalism

A. Origins

The beginning of Pentecostalism is often said to be the spiritual experience of Agnes N. Ozman at the Methodist Bethel Bible School of Charles Fox Parham in Topeka, Kansas. She had this experience on January 1, 1901, at 11 o'clock at night.[258] I cannot refrain from pointing out that this was the same time when Pope Leo XIII consecrated the world to the Holy Spirit. Agnes Ozman spoke in tongues—in the Chinese language, which she did not know at all.[259] I tend to think that this was a prophecy regarding the spread of Christianity in China. In what follows I heavily rely on the book written by Frank Bartleman in 1925 in Los Angeles, *How Pentecost Came to Los Angeles*, republished in 1980 as *Azusa Street*, with an introduction by Vinson Synan.[260] Apart from the introduction, the book describes Bartleman's reminiscences of how he experienced the origins of the Pentecostal movement in the United States. Bartleman dedicated the book "to the many precious souls who with the author were privileged in seeing and experiencing the early days of blessing of the 'Latter Rain' outpouring at the old 'power house,' Azusa Street Mission. It is written with the hope and prayer that, where lost, the vision may be renewed to those who once shared with us in the glory of this 'former house' of blessing; and also that it may, through this humble little medium, be told 'to the generation following.'"[261]

The essential tenants of faith of the initial congregation led by the African-American William J. Seymour were: (1) justification by faith, (2) sanctification as a clear work of grace, (3) Baptism in the Holy Spirit, the first sign of which was speaking in tongues, (4) divine healing as 'being contained in the atoning death of Christ,' and (5) bodily rapture of the believers before the thousand-year reign at the second coming of Christ.[262] Starting in April of 1906, the congregation gathered in an old building on Azusa Street in Los Angeles.[263] Both before and after the events of Azusa, Bartleman was active in other churches, and he contributed to various newspapers and books.

Regarding the five articles of faith, one needs to say the following. About (2): The teaching of sanctification comes from the Methodists, more specifically, from John Wesley who derived it from Anglican Franciscans with Catholic roots. Wesley came across this teaching among the German Pietists. He started to have problems with Zinzendorf when the latter turned away from the teaching of sanctification, moving closer to Lutheranism.[264] About (3): It is not specified how one reaches the Baptism in the Holy Spirit. About (4): As Paul makes clear, divine healing is not to be taken for granted.[265] One of the main reasons for divine healing is to convince unbelievers of the faith. Typical examples are the evangelistic meetings of Hathaway, Bonnke, etc. About (5) The concept of the "bodily rapture" is not quite clear. Until about 1830, it was obvious to most that the rapture would take place when the Lord returned to establish his 'thousand-year' reign—after the time of the great tribulation (cf. Mt 24:3-50,[266] esp. 30f.; Mk 13 , esp. 24f.; Lk 21:5-36, esp. 25f.). The rapture was seen as simply a transformation of people's mortal bodies into immortal bodies (after those who died have been raised bodily from the dead), and a meeting[267] in the clouds of the coming Lord who returns with the clouds the same way he left before Pentecost. This is in line with the Israelite view and is also said by the virgins who are waiting for the Lord at the wedding.[268] The clouds are an area that still belongs to the earth. Those who have been raptured return with the Lord to the earth where they will rule together for a "thousand" years in their immortal bodies, together with those raised from the dead. This, they do independently of whether they were protected or died during the time of tribulation.

We do not want to suppress the fact that some people today interpret the rapture to mean that believers, by being raptured, will be protected from the coming tribulation, which would mean that the second coming of Christ might come in two stages.

Others expect this to happen in the middle of the tribulation. I wonder whether these theories might not be fueled by the thought that believers should be protected, even though those who died will be raised to live with the Lord and martyrs have repeatedly produced new believers. We, too, live at a time when Christians are being greatly persecuted in many places, yet Christianity is also spreading like never before.

In his first chapter, Bartleman describes how he dedicated his life to God. "I promised the rest of my life should be spent wholly for Him. He made a fresh covenant with me."[269] Bartleman had already given his life to Jesus at an earlier stage, and now the death of his little daughter Esther caused him to renew this commitment. He realized that the time after death was much more important than the time before death.

Bartleman also speaks of having "repented." He says, "We must keep humble and little in our own eyes." And: "The depth of any revival will be determined exactly by the spirit of repentance it obtains. In fact this is the key to every true revival born of God."[270] Not only in this point does Bartleman have a very closer affinity to Sister Mary of the Divine Heart.[271] In the second chapter, he says, "Like the full moon that draws clearer and nearer to our vision as we continue to steadfastly gaze at it, so Jesus appears more real to our souls as we continue to contemplate Him. We need a closer, personal, vital relationship, acquaintance, and communion with God."[272] This sounds very much like the devotion to the Sacred Heart of Jesus.

Finally, there was also much prayer at the genesis of the Pentecostal movement. This usually happened at the altar at the end of services,[273] which was where they started praying for an outpouring of the Holy Spirit in Los Angeles and the whole of southern California.[274] Further, Bartleman recounts a very special encounter with the Lord, which I can only convey in his own words:

"One evening, July 3, I felt strongly impressed to go to the little Peniel Hall in Pasadena to pray. There I found Brother Boehmer ahead of me. He had also been led of God to the hall. We prayed for a spirit of revival for Pasadena until the burden became well nigh unbearable. I cried out like a woman in birth-pangs. The Spirit was interceding through us. Finally the burden left us. After a little time of quiet waiting a great calm settled down upon us. Then suddenly, without premonition, the Lord Jesus himself revealed himself to us. He seemed to stand directly between us, so close we could have reached out our hand and touched him. But we did not dare to move. I could not even look. In fact I seemed all spirit. His presence seemed more real, if possible, than if I could have seen and touched Him naturally. I forgot I had eyes or ears. My spirit recognized Him. A heaven of divine love filled and thrilled my soul. Burning fire went through me. In fact my whole being seemed to flow down before Him, like wax before the fire. I lost all consciousness of time or space, being conscious only of His wonderful presence. I worshipped at His feet. It seemed a veritable 'mount of transfiguration.' I was lost in the pure Spirit.

For some time He remained with us. Then slowly He withdrew His presence. We would have been there yet had He not withdrawn. I could not doubt His reality after that experience. Brother Boehmer experienced largely the same thing. We had lost all consciousness of each other's presence while He remained with us. We were almost afraid to speak or breathe when we came back to our surroundings. The Lord had said nothing to us, but only ravished our spirits by His presence. He had come to strengthen and assure us for His service. We knew now we were workers with Him, fellowshippers of his sufferings, in the ministry of 'soul travail.' Real soul travail is just as definite in the spirit, as natural human birth-pangs. The simile is almost perfect in its sameness. No soul is ever born without this. All true revivals of salvation come this way."[275]

Here, I want to come back to the point that the Pentecostal teaching today says that the basis for the Baptism with the Holy Spirit is prayer, obedience, and having given one's life to the Lord. Obedience, however, should not be seen as keeping what the Bible commands through intellectual understanding and willpower. Rather, it is a Spirit-led obedience that comes from the heart. It is a repentance that may often be tearful.

Bartleman also suffered much from sickness and financial lack. Yet, God always prevented the worst. He felt like he was realizing a little of what Paul meant about "filling up the cup of His sufferings" for a lost world.[276] But then he added, "Our Lord was a 'man of sorrows,' as well as of joy."[277]

More than half a century earlier, there was a ten-year-old girl who was dying, until the people gathered around her "began to hear the most entrancing strains of music, manifestly not of this world, coming from the distance. It rapidly approached, becoming more audible, until it finally ceased for a time just over the house where they were gathered. The child's face lit up with a very halo of glory, and as the presence of God filled the room they realized that a band of heavenly beings encompassed them, and as they seemed almost to hear the rustle of angels' wings, the spirit of the little one passed out of its temple of clay, in a rapture of transcending joy. The heavenly music was again resumed, and soon died away in the distance."[278]

"From John Wesley's diary we gather the following, under date of March 29, 1782: 'Being Good Friday, I came to Mansfield to assist in the services of the day. While we were administering the sacrament to about thirteen hundred people I heard a low, soft, solemn sound, just like that of an aeolian harp. It continued five or six minutes, and so affected many that they could not refrain from tears. It then gradually died away.'"[279]

The Pentecostal movement added something new to such experiences. In addition to speaking in tongues there was also "singing in the Spirit," a heavenly song that produced such rapture that it could not be put into words.[280] It was a "new song." Sometimes, Bartleman writes, it was a song without words, sometimes a singing in tongues. "It brought a heavenly atmosphere, as though the angels themselves were present and joining with us."[281] Bartleman also relates an event that happened in a "New Testament church" in which the people sang in this manner while lying on the floor.[282]

Of course, there was also normal singing in theses churches, but Bartleman says that this can actually hinder the spirit of repentance.[283] Nor is he at all happy about many of the normal church songs at the time. He says that there is very little real spirit of worship in them. They move the toes, but not the hearts of people.[284]

According to him, everything in the Pentecostal gatherings happened spontaneously, led by the Spirit. They were free of any kind of priesthood or the misuse of spiritual hierarchy.[285] There was no priestly caste, nor a priestly profession. All these things came later, when the movement was already going downhill.[286] Usually, Brother Seymour sat behind two empty shoe boxes, one on top of the other, and he kept his head inside the top one during the meeting, praying.[287] People who came to the meetings tried to avoid any human contact and greetings. They first wanted to meet God. They got their head under some bench in the corner and prayed.[288]

B. Biblical Clues

There are several passages in the Bible that point to Christians who do not belong to the Catholic Church—that is, to the woman in the wilderness—because they do not have any ordained members among their midst.

As mentioned before, the time of the woman in the wilderness is predicted to be limited. But there are more passages that are relevant:

(1) First of all, there is he passage where the Apostle John complains about people who used the name of Jesus to heal the sick and drive out demons without being part of the apostles. In response, the Lord rebukes John with the word: Those who are not against me are for me.[289]

(2) There is also an interesting prophecy of the risen Lord about the apostles Peter and John: "When they had finished breakfast, Jesus said to Simon Peter, 'Simon, son of John, do you love me more than these?' He said to him, 'Yes, Lord, you know that I love you.' He said to him, 'Feed my lambs.'" This was repeated three times. And then Jesus said, "Amen, amen, I say to you, when you were younger, you used to dress yourself and go where you wanted; but when you grow old, you will stretch out your hands, and someone else will dress you and lead you where you do not want to go." And when he had said this, he said to him, "Follow me." The Apostle John interprets this to mean that Jesus predicted with what kind of death Peter would glorify God, that is, by being crucified. But the choice of words is rather vague, suggesting that Jesus also wants to predict something else. Also, the time contrast of "when you were younger" and "when you grow old" does not quite fit the crucifixion. This leads me to the conclusion that the prophecy has another, more far-

reaching, meaning: it is about Peter, the Rock, whose successors would be the bishops and popes of Rome, taking up his role. The instruction to "tend my sheep" is even more applicable to them than to him. And the phrasing "when you grow old" gains a historical meaning. In fact, Peter's successors in Rome would stretch out their hands, that is, would gain worldwide influence. And someone else would dress them and lead them: Jesus himself, who determines the succession of Peter and reveals to them what is to be determined in questions of dogma and ethics. However, the reference to being dressed by someone else might also refer to a future papal election that turns away from Rome and establishes the papal seat somewhere else, possibly in Jerusalem. This could mean a restructuring of the papacy that might include Pentecostals.

(3) After Jesus said to Peter, "Follow me," Peter turned and saw the disciple whom Jesus loved. It is expressly said that this was the disciple who had reclined upon Jesus' chest during the supper. Let us recall the conversation that Gertrude of Helfta had with this disciple.[291] Of this disciple, Jesus now says in answer to Peter, "What if I want him to remain until I come? What concern is it of yours? You follow me." Here, too, it might be appropriate to speak of the type that this disciple symbolizes and see a historical prediction in this, as John resembles the Pentecostals described by Bartleman. His spirituality is based more on having given his life to Christ—as in the devotion to the Sacred Heart of Jesus—than on the Eucharist, which he does not even describe.

By devoting his life in this way to Jesus, John takes the suffering and death of Christ into himself. It is he who stands under the cross at the key moment, together with Mary, the mother of the Lord. Perhaps it is also possible to connect this to the fact that his brother James was the first of the twelve disciples who was killed as a result of having followed Jesus, by Herod Agrippa I,[292] although only after the deacon Stephen had already been stoned to death by Jews. James, by being a martyr, took part in the sacrifice of Christ and, through it, might also represent the soul of his brother John who died on the inside for Jesus. When Herod saw that the death of James pleased the Jews, he also arrested Peter, with the goal of killing him as well, but God freed Peter, as the time of his death had not yet come. Later, however, he did die on the cross, thus also turning into a kind of John—which once more can be interpreted as relating to the papacy. It should also be mentioned that Christians protected the remains of James from the Mohammedans, who did not believe that Christ was the Son of God and died on the cross, and, even less, that he brought salvation to a sinful humanity. Their God, Allah, in his absolute unity and sovereignty, has no relationship to his believers who can never be sure whether they will go to "heaven," which, incidentally, is supposed to be completely earthly in character. Across northern Africa, the remains of James were successively brought away from the Mohammedans, ending up in Spain where they were kept safe in the far northeast, in Compostela. Nowhere else have there been—nor are today—so many pilgrims from all over Europe as those who come to "Santiago di Compostela." It is a place that is more important than Tours or Poitiers in France where the attacking Mohammedans were defeated. In Santioago, the false faith of the Mohammedans has been negated.

A final consideration is that Jesus called James and John the "sons of thunder,"[239] just like he called Peter "rock," that is, "Kephas" or "Peter."[294] I interpret "sons of thunder" like this: Christ is the lightning from heaven, and the thunder is the effect that follows on the earth. Just like Catholics take the reference to Peter being the "rock" and apply it to his successors, using it as a foundation for the Church, in the same manner, the term "sons of thunder" can be applied to the successors of John and James. Their father is not so much Zebedee but, in a wider sense, Christ himself. The disciples with the nicknames Rock and Sons of Thunder were the only ones who witnessed the Transfiguration of Jesus. There, they came in contact with the past (Elijah and Moses) and, presumably, would also have significance for the future.[295]

(4) We now need to turn to the 144,000 who are foretold in Revelation. We already discussed how the Pentecostal movement is the true day of the Holy Spirit after the Pentecost evening before. The first Pentecostals, as well as many later Pentecostals, also talked about the latter rain in the sense in which the other James and Joel talk about it.[297] Another picture is the removal of the woman in the wilderness who is only taken care of there for a limited time. Something else that might be

relevant in this connection is the 144,000 in Revelation 14:1-5 who are mentioned right after the woman in the wilderness. I know that this number is often applied to all who go to heaven. But the Pentecostal Bartleman also speaks of singing a "new song" during his time in Los Angeles.[298] This is a reference to the 144,000.

The following is the whole text regarding the 144,000:

"(1) Then I looked and there was the Lamb standing on Mount Zion, and with him a hundred and forty-four thousand who had his name and his Father's name written on their foreheads. (2) I heard a sound from heaven like the sound of rushing water or a loud peal of thunder. The sound I heard was like that of harpists playing their harps. (3) They were singing (what seemed to be) a new hymn before the throne, before the four living creatures and the elders. No one could learn this hymn except the hundred and forty-four thousand who had been ransomed from the earth. (4) These are they who were not defiled with women; they are virgins and these are the ones who follow the Lamb wherever he goes. They have been ransomed as the firstfruits of the human race for God and the Lamb. (5) On their lips no deceit has been found; they are unblemished."

The 144,000 correspond to the woman in the wilderness who has a crown of twelve stars on her head.[299] Both numbers refer to the twelve apostles. 144 is the square number of 12. Both symbolize a form of the church and both stand for an apostolic church. The apostolicity of the woman is that the twelve apostles passed on the blessing of the Holy Spirit to later generations in a successive manner through the ordination of the presbyter (elders). The 144,000 are believers who took in and passed on what the apostles had said and written. Apart from that, they have a close relationship with the Lamb, that is, with the Son of God and God the Father. They sing a "new hymn/song," accompanied by heavenly harps. It is reminiscent of the singing in tongues of the first Pentecostals in Los Angeles. The 144,000 have been ransomed as a result of their faith—they have been taken from the earth, have not defiled themselves with women, they are virgins, without deceit, unblemished. They follow the Lord. One should not take such descriptions too literally, though. What they communicate is the "separateness" of these people;

their soul is not attached to this world, and if they had not died and risen with Christ, they would kill themselves or immerse themselves in drugs. I know this from personal experience. When I was fifteen, the meaninglessness of life drove me to despair, and I thought about committing suicide. Then, it seems, the Holy Spirit gave me the thought that I could at least watch my life. I only became a true believer seven years later, but this sense of being detached from life in this world was already an important foundation for me.

There is still something else to be said about the number 144,000. It was an old Egyptian idea to see square numbers in more universal ways. The triad, for instance, was a symbol of a certain divinity. The Egyptian language did not only differentiate between singular and plural but singular, dyad, and triad. The triad not only meant three but could stand for an infinite number. That is why the number three symbolized infinity, which made it the number of a divinity. When one wanted to symbolize not a certain god but divinity in general, one squared three. The gods of a locale were called the Holy Ennead ("Holy Nine"), no matter how many gods there actually were. The number of the earth was of course four, because of the four cardinal directions. The Greek Pythagoras was educated in Egypt and brought home not only the equation $3^2 + 4^2 = 5^2$ for the right-angled triangle but also the symbolic Egyptian interpretations of such numbers. Five is the number of the god-man Pharaoh. His pyramid has five corners, triangular sides and a rectangular base. These same numbers were used in the early church. The number for the God-man Jesus is five, and not only because of the five wounds. Originally, there were also five patriarchies in the church. (Unfortunately, there are some Evangelicals today who have no appreciation anymore for such equivocal meanings of numbers.) The multiplication with thousand is of course meant to emphasize the great number of believers.[300]

(5) The reference to the latter rain can be interpreted in the same way, especially by cross-referencing it to Joel where it is foretold that the Holy Spirit would be poured out over all believers.[301] Rain is a picture for spiritual gifts (Isa 55:10f; Hos 6:3; 10:12). It is also noteworthy that the former rain (*yorah*) takes place in October and the latter rain (*malkhosch*)

in March/April (Deut 11:14; Job 29:23; Pr 16,15; Jer 3:3; 5,24; Hos 6,3; Joel 2:23; Zech 10:1).[302]

C. Background

The origins of Pentecostalism in the United States are rooted in England. Synan[303] specifically mentions the Methodist Holiness movement, the Catholic Apostolic movement of Eduard Irving, and the British Keswick Higher Life movement. The most important of these was the Holiness movement, which grew out of Methodism in the eighteenth century. The Anglican priest John Wesley experienced an evangelical renewal in 1738. He declared that he had felt his heart strangely warmed and called this a "rebirth." Pentecostals also adopted Wesley's teaching of a "second blessing," which is supposed to come as a result of a crisis subsequent to being saved. He called it "complete sanctification," "perfect love," "Christian perfection" or "purity of the heart." Wesley's colleague, John Fletcher, was the first who called this the "Baptism in the Holy Spirit," an experience that endowed believers with spiritual power and cleansed them from within. In the nineteenth century, Robert Irving and his friends proclaimed that the modern church might experience a renewal of the gifts of the Spirit. In 1831, this Presbyterian pastor tried to initiate a Charismatic renewal in his Presbyterian church, later developing the Catholic Apostolic Church. There were tongues and prophecies, but the experiences did not turn into a wider movement. Eventually, after 1875 there arose the Keswick Higher Life Movement in England. Spurred on by American Holiness preachers, they soon reinterpreted Wesley's "second blessing," which had been mostly concerned about purifying the heart, turning it into a "gift of spiritual power for ministry." Dwight Lyman Moody, too, was part of this movement.

In the United States, Pentecostalism grew out of such Holiness movements. The only thing that was added was the gift of tongues as a sign of the second blessing. The first Pentecostals were the people in Parham's Bible school in Topeka, Kansas, in 1901. Parham formulated the teaching that speaking in tongues was the "biblical evidence" of the Baptism in the Holy Spirit.[304] Parham called his movement "Apostolic faith."[305] Then, in 1906,, the movement in Los Angeles started on Azusa Street, under the leadership of the African-American William Joseph Seymour who had learned about the Baptism in the Holy Spirit with tongues in 1905 at a Bible school that Parham led in Houston, Texas. From Azusa Street, Pentecostalism spread throughout the world, first slowly but then, after the Second World War, with increasing visibility. Wherever it spread, it became obvious that Pentecostals emphasized: definite conversion, a holy life through separation from the world, and the "Baptism in the Holy Spirit," which was evidenced by speaking in tongues. After believers experienced this Baptism, the gifts of the Spirit would become a normal part of church life. What was particularly emphasized was divine healing as an answer to prayer, as well as the second coming of Christ with a "rapture" of the church, which could happen any time. Typical was also very joyful and expressive worship, which seemed emotional and noisy to outsiders on first witnessing it. There was raising of hands, loud praising of God, speaking in tongues, interpretation of tongues, prophecies, prayer for the sick, and, occasionally, exorcisms. Fiery, Bible-oriented preaching proclaimed salvation, holiness, healing and material blessing for all who prayed fervently at the altar. What made the greatest impression was the teaching that the gifts of the Spirit (also called the *charismata*) were meant for the twentieth century just as much as for the early church in the first century.

The Church of God in Christ (COGIC), whose predominately African-American members had been freed from slavery only a generation before, caught the fire of the Pentecostal movement. Today (in 2001), it has six million members in more than 15,000 churches. In 1914, the Assemblies of God (AG) were founded in Chicago. In 2001, this movement has more than two million members in the United States and forty-four million in 150 other countries. In 1916, so-called Oneness Pentecostalism split off the AG, teaching that God was only one Person and the names of the Father, the Son, and the Holy Spirit were only titles invented by the Roman Catholic Church.

Chapter 7

The Development of Pentecostalism

A. Spirituality

As demonstrated, one of the roots of the Pentecostal movement is John Wesley who, after experiencing salvation, also experienced a second blessing and sanctification. Thereafter, he founded Methodism, out of which later grew the Holiness movement. It was in that movement, in Chicago, that William Durham experienced the third blessing of being baptized in the Holy Spirit, accompanied by speaking in tongues. This led Durham to advocate a teaching that he called the "finished work of Calvary." According to it, sanctification already began with salvation, but it was a growing process. This teaching, however, caused a split in the Pentecostal movement, because leaders like Parham (1873–1929) and Seymour did not accept it. Added to this was the fact that Pentecostals who had a Baptist, Presbyterian or another Reformed background had problems with the doctrine of sanctification anyway.

With thirty-five million members worldwide (2001), the Assemblies of God (AG) is the largest and most well-known Classic Pentecostal association in the world. It also has the most influential and visible Pentecostal public body, which demands respect in the wider circle of Evangelical and Charismatic Christians.

While Pentecostals who came out of the Holiness movement usually advocated the "second blessing" theory, newer organizations such as the Assemblies of God left the question open or accepted the "finished work" view. Today, this is the view shared by most American

Pentecostals. In this way, Pentecostalism has distanced itself spiritually from Classical Protestantism. Luther is said to have taught that justification is a judicial act through which God justifies sinners even if they remain unrighteous and sinful on the inside.[307] It is not a renewal and sanctification from within but merely an outward imputation of the righteousness of Christ. The requirement for this justification is the so-called *fiducial* faith, that is, the confidence of the believer that God, being merciful, forgives him his sins for the sake of Christ. In contrast, in response to the Reformation, the Council of Trent made clear that faith always led to a supernatural sanctification and renewal of the inner man.[308] In effect, the sinful man dies with Jesus Christ and, together with him, is reborn as a new, sinless man.[309] This is the dogmatic, theological belief. It is what is illustrated in the Bible through the anointing with the nard oil from the alabaster jar and of which Jesus said that it would always be mentioned wherever the Gospel was going to be preached.[310] To be effective, this faith requires the works of love.[311] Even when sin is no longer present, negative consequences can remain in the human soul, which are often healed only through a slow process of sanctification. In Catholicism, they are known as "punishment for one's sins or consequenses of sins."

The agreement of the spiritual teaching of Pentecostalism with Catholicism as opposed to the Classical Protestant teaching came across clearly in the official talks between Catholics and Pentecostals that, starting in 1972, have repeatedly taken place.[312]

In the second dialogue session (1973), David du Plessis declared[313] "that Pentecostalism did not belong to Protestantism, nor was it a split-off of the Protestant church, but a completely new movement that was based on the experiences of rebirth and the Baptism in the Holy Spirit."[314] Vinson Synan, in the press report of the second session, also cites, "The best of the modern Pentecostal movement has much in common with the highest and best in the Catholic mystical tradition as seen in the holy and charismatic lives of the saints."[315] Also of note is the observation by Heribert Mühlen: "All Christians are called and enabled to mystical experiences of the divine mystery, though there are different degrees of intensity. The same is true of Charismatic experiences. The release today of charismata among individual believers is a new epoch of church history."[316] Mühlen also wrote a book entitled *Entsakralisierung* ("Desacralization"), which basically points to the end of the wilderness woman through the spread of the 144,000.

B. The Five Problems of Pentecostalism

1. Evangelicalism

The basis of Pentecostal theology is part of "Evangelicalism," which believes in the reliability of the Bible as the "Word of God." It is not quite clear what exactly this means, though. There are very different interpretations. This focus of Evangelicalism originally came about in the nineteenth century as "Fundamentalism," which was a reaction against the liberal Protestantism with its Bible-critical, modernist orientation.[317] Starting in the 1920s, the extreme form of Fundamentalism experienced a less narrow-hearted continuation in the form of Evangelicalism. Fundamentalists did not only reject Catholic interpretation of the Bible but also the acknowledgment of miracles throughout church history. They claimed that miracles had finished when the text of the Bible had been completed. By taking this position, they also turned against the growing Pentecostal movement. As we shall still see, many Pentecostals adopted the teaching of the Fundamentalist John Nelson Darby regarding the rapture within the framework of millennialism. An important Evangelical leader was Billy Graham.[318] In Europe, Evangelicals founded the "Evangelical Alliance," which, among other things, emphasized the inspiration of the Bible.[319]

What precisely Evangelicalism means for the Pentecostal movement today cannot be easily determined. I have taken two books as a basis: *Foundations of Pentecostal Theology* by Guy P. Duffield and Nathaniel M. Van Cleave (English version, 1983) and the Fire Bible, formerly known as the Full Life Study Bible, which was first published in 1990 (New Testament) and 1992 (full Bible). In both of these texts, I have looked at the commentaries to the creation account in Genesis.[320] In Duffield,[321] it basically says that the Holy Scriptures are not just an inspiration by the Holy Spirit of the authors of the Bible—which might make room for human error—but a direct agency of God, determining the result of the Bible.[322] However, it is emphasized that the Bible is right in moral and spiritual matters, leaving open the question of other topics.[323] When one reads the exposition on creation,[324] there is a degree of elasticity.[325] It says that a more detailed analysis of certain statements should be left to comments on the topic of "science and the Bible." It goes on to say that conservatives do not all agree and some modern scientists admit that there is no conflict between Genesis 1 and the known facts of science today.[326] I can add here that there are professors who are not believers and yet expressly reject the theories of Darwin.[327]

In the Fire Bible, it says about Genesis 1:7[328] that a day of creation does not have to be understood as a period of twenty-four hours. The article about creation is along the same lines, or at least without contradiction to it.[329]

On the other hand, I have attended a Pentecostal congregation in which a younger preacher said that the days of creation were really twenty-four-hour periods.

Finally, by way of comparison, I would like to point out the Catholic teaching in this regard. Today, it is expressed *in The Dogmatic Constitution on Divine Revelation* of the Second Vatican Council: "It is common knowledge that among all the Scriptures, even those of the New Testament, the Gospels have a special preeminence, and rightly so, for they are the principal witness for the life and teaching of the incarnate Word, our savior."[330] "Therefore Christ the Lord … commissioned the Apostles to preach to all men that Gospel which is the source of all saving truth and moral teaching."[331] Hence, there are two basic principles: (1) The entire Bible is to be interpreted in light of the four Gospels. This is made clear in Catholic services. Every time, in addition to a text from the Old Testament and/or a letter from the New Testament, there is also always a text from the Gospels. While the other texts are read by a layperson and the congregation remains seated, the text from the Gospels is read by a priest (or deacon), often framed by singing Hallelujah and read from a special Gospel book with a golden cover, and the congregation stands up during the entire reading. (2) Only statements in the Bible about God (theology) and morality are binding. Statements about nature do not have anything to do with questions of faith, making it irrelevant whether they are true. This means that the word *day* in the creation account can be seen in a broader sense as any time period, no matter how long. After all, on the first "day," both day and night are created, and the seventh day lasts from the creation of man until Jesus Christ, the second Adam. The church has always taught that, with him, the eighth day has started, which has no end. That is why we no longer celebrate the Sabbath (Saturday) but Sunday, and actually every day is a Sunday.

2. The Oneness Pentecostals

Early on within Pentecostalism, there was a movement that rejected baptism in the name of the Father, the Son and the Holy Spirit, advocating instead a baptism in the name of Jesus alone.[332] They appealed to a rather fundamentalist interpretation of the Bible. Inspired by the Old Testament, they thought the name of God was important: Yeshuah = Yahweh is salvation.[333] They also based their view on Peter's invitation on Pentecost: "Repent and be baptized, every one of you, in the name of Jesus Christ for the forgiveness of your sins; and you will receive the gift of the holy Spirit."[334] For this reason, they also believed that everything happened at baptism and that no further Spirit baptism was needed. Finally, they rejected the Trinity of the three Persons of God, demanding that those who had been baptized in the name of all three Persons should be baptized again according to the Oneness view. Their position is a typical case of a too literal and one-sided interpretation of the Bible. They criticize orthodox theology for supposedly denying the oneness of God, but they only do so because people in modern times have forgotten the ancient teachings on the nature of being. According to these ancient teachings, the three Persons of God do not only have the same being—also called *substance* or *nature*—but a so-called consubstantiality. The three Persons are one in the *perichoresis* or *circumincessio*; each Person is found in the other, like Jesus saying that he was in the Father and the Father in him. Oneness Pentecostals, however, reject Trinitarian theology as "Catholic."

In 1916, the Oneness Pentecostals split off from the Assemblies of God. 156 of 585 ministers lost their membership. Leading up to this step, the Assemblies of God accepted a "Statement of Fundamental Truths," consisting of seventeen points, in which the doctrine of the Trinity was clearly confirmed.[335] What is interesting is that, originally, Pentecostals wanted to only acknowledge the Bible as the basis of faith, to be interpreted under the leadership of the Holy Spirit, without listing any dogma that were to be interpreted. But obviously this was not possible.

3. The Teaching of the Rapture

Before the second coming, which was announced by the angel at the Ascension of Christ, there will be a time of tribulation, bringing with it the Antichrist and the wrath of God.[336] Now, John Nelson Darby (1800–1882) taught that before Christ returns to the earth there will be a "rapture." That is, he thought Christ would take the glorified bodies of the deceased and still living believers to himself into heaven where they would be safe. Depending on the different variations of the teaching which developed later, this could happen either at the beginning of the Tribulation, in the middle, or right before the "wrath of God."

This teaching is to be rejected. In the Geneva Study Bible,[337] it states briefly that this cannot be reconciled with what the Bible actually says. Prior to Darby in 1830, this teaching did not exist. Darby came from the Plymouth Brethren, which had split off Edward Irving (1792–1834). Going more into the detail of the text, the word used in First Thessalonians 4:12 actually means "come to meet" or "pick up." The believers go to the clouds to "pick up" Jesus, returning to earth right away. This is his second coming, arriving to stay for a thousand years. The word in question (*apantesis*) is also used when Jesus speaks of the ten virgins meeting the groom to go to the wedding, and when Paul speaks of being picked up by the Roman believers on his way to Rome.[338]

The notion that the church would be protected from the Tribulation on earth contradicts everything that has happened in the past: the church has never grown as much as in times of persecution. This was true of pre-Constantinian times, and it is still true. Stephen saw the heavens open when he was stoned,[339] surely experiencing the joy of heaven within himself. This is something all true martyrs experience. They make the cross of Christ real to people, leading many to the faith.

Also, there is no reason why those who died should be bodily raised and raptured to heaven, as their souls are already with the Lord.[340] They are no longer subject to earthly pain.

Now, it is true that the sun will darken and that the moon will not give its light.[341] This is Christ and the church. But this only applies to unbelievers. Believers still see the sun and shine themselves.

It is significant that this kind of "rapture" cannot be found in books such as *The New International Dictionary of Pentecostal Movements* by Burgess, *The Century of the Holy Spirit* by Synan and the Fire Bible by Stamps, yet it is thoroughly treated in *Pentecostal Theology* by Duffield.

4. Asceticism: Fasting, Poverty, Chastity, Obedience

(a) Praying and Fasting

It is reported that the first Christians also fasted while praying.[342] On the other hand, Jesus condemned the legalistic fasting of Jews, especially when it was done for show, and he called people who were fasting to dress and act in a way that others would not even know they were fasting.[343]

One has to realize that fasting is not just an outward act to show deference for God but influences both body and soul, strengthening our relationship with God. It is a kind of asceticism that promotes mysticism. Normally, the soul looks to the body to receive nourishment, but the body looks for nourishment for itself. When a person fasts, the body is no longer able to give the soul anything. The soul has to look elsewhere, which means it opens up to the spiritual world. There, it can meet either God or Satan. Esoterics know this too. Fasting can bring you in contact with evil spirits, but faith in Jesus Christ protects us from this. He is the gate to the kingdom of God, and it is through him that we pray.

The forty-day fast of the Lord after being baptized and filled with the Spirit demonstrates this situation quite clearly.[344] It says explicitly that the Lord was led by the Holy Spirit into the wilderness. This implies that it was the Spirit who caused him to fast. But, as is typical in these situations, he was not only filled with the Spirit of God but also came into contact with the Devil. When the Devil tempted him to turn the stones of the wilderness into bread—since he was, after all, the Son of God—he replied, "One does not live by bread alone, but by every word that comes forth from the mouth of God." This shows clearly that a person's soul turns to God when it does not get any bread, and that it can be nourished by God. One may think of Saint Nicholas of Flüe who did not eat or drink for nineteen years but obviously received a special grace of God for doing so.[345] On the other hand, the Lord said that his disciples did not fast as long as he was with them, but only when he was gone.[346] This could also apply to believers in whom Christ is born.

(b) Poverty, Chastity and Obedience: The Evangelical Counsels

Poverty, chastity and obedience have long formed part of the life of a monk or nun. In the Catholic Church, these are called the "evangelical counsels."[347]

α) Poverty

There are a great number of passages in the Bible that deal with poverty, the most important and central of which is the first beatitude: "Blessed are the poor in spirit, for theirs is the kingdom of heaven."[348] Poor in spirit is usually interpreted to mean spiritual poverty: a low estimation of oneself and sometimes even a lack of being filled with the Holy Spirit. That is why some translations—departing from the Greek original—translate the verse as saying "those who are poor in the sight of God." But I think it means not to cling to the things of this world and our possessions, and definitely not to have ambition for material wealth. This is what makes us willing to share with the poor whatever wealth God has given us.[349] What is important is to have as though we did not have. As Paul explains, "I tell you, brothers, the time is running out. From now on, let those having wives act as not having them, those weeping as not weeping, those rejoicing as not rejoicing, those buying as not owning, those using the world as not using it fully. For the world in its present form is passing away."[350] The parallel passage in Luke omits the addition "in the spirit": "Blessed are you who are poor, for the kingdom of God is yours."[351] This leaves open the question whether one is actually poor or just poor on the inside in the sense of being detached from possessions.

It is characteristic that this poverty is mentioned as a prerequisite for the kingdom of heaven, as a basis for mysticism. Poverty in which one suffers from the desire for riches can be a first step at the most, similar to the feeling of hunger when fasting.

β) Chastity

Chastity is not primarily about the renunciation of erotic relationships but also about a marriage relationship that is blessed by God, with view of having children. It is a reflection of the relationship of Christ to the believers.[352] The purpose here is not primarily to discuss marriage but the chastity and celibacy of monks and nuns as well as of priests in the Catholic and Orthodox Church.[353] It is a fact that, according to old church teaching, fasting also always includes sexual chastity.[354] Since fasting is a preparation for prayer, opening people up to God, it has never been desirable for priests—who need to pray a lot—to be married. Otherwise, there could also be unreasonable demands put on the wife. This is the reason the Orthodox Church, though allowing married men to be ordained as priests, has not allowed unmarried priests to marry. This led to many future priests to marry shortly before ordination, which is why the Catholic West stopped ordaining married men altogether. In the East, too, a married priest cannot become a bishop. On the other hand, Anglican priests in more recent times who converted to Catholicism (because the Anglican Church introduced the priesthood for women) continued to be accepted as priests even if they were married.

P. Meinrad Gyr S. J. teaches the following about marriage: "According to Ephesians 5, the marriage sacrament is a sign of the covenant between Christ and his church. … In marriage, one lives in a symbolic way what virginity achieves in a more direct way. … It is a similar situation as with blood baptism. Water baptism is a sign that a person is being taken up into the death and resurrection of Christ. Blood baptism, in contrast, is a direct unification with the dying and raised Christ. It is not a sign but that to which the sign points."[355] Today, one might call this a "realization" of the cross of Christ. P. Meinrad Gyr takes the view that Mary, as the mother of the Lord, stands both for the relationship of Jesus to the believers as well as for sacramental marriage.[356] I would like to add that, due to his connection to the divine, the chaste believer receives Christ who grows in him, enabling him to say together with Paul, "I have been crucified with Christ; yet I live, no longer I, but Christ lives in me."[357] The Lord is actually born in us, as the German mystics of medieval times taught.

γ) Obedience

First of all, this is not about obedience to God but obedience of children to their parents; wives to their husbands; servants to their masters;[358] church members to their leaders and elders;[359] and all to the government.[360] Apart from the fact that, as a rule, obedience is necessary for the world to function, it is a practice in humility. We also need this humility to obey God, who wants to lead us with his Spirit. Only when we have practiced obedience can we listen to the Spirit. In actual fact, though, obedience to God is true freedom that makes us happy. God has created us, and that is why he knows better than we do what serves our well-being. It is not only Jesus Christ who could say, "My food is to do the will of the one who sent me";[361] it is something that is true of all believers. It is through obedience to the Holy Spirit that we are being filled with bliss. Admittedly, one may ask where Jesus' happiness was when he realized that obedience to the Father meant going to the cross, and of course the same question may be asked about any believers who are being led by the Spirit into situations that cause them harm. Outwardly, a situation might really be unhappy, but this is always connected to blessedness in one's heart. Stephen saw the heaven open when he was stoned for his faith,[362] and he surely already experienced some of the heavenly bliss. The bliss that our Father in heaven has planned for us is not of this world but meant for eternity, of which we can already have a foretaste in this world. It is not without reason that he says, "Take my yoke upon you and learn from me, for I am meek and humble of heart; and you will find rest for your selves. For my yoke is easy, and my burden light."[363] Already in the Old Testament, it says in Psalm 23: "… to still waters he leads me; he restores my soul. … You set a table before me in front of my enemies."[364]

Among Pentecostals, there is the tendency to neglect these counsels, reducing the element of mysticism.

Chapter 8

Doctrine: Positive Confession (5)

There is a teaching that is variably called "positive confession," "Word of Faith teaching," "faith movement," word-faith," "faith-formula theology," "prosperity doctrine," "faith churches," etc.[365]

Kenneth L. Hagin Sr. (1917–2003) is generally considered the founder of this movement.[366] He was not a Pentecostal, though, instead following in the footsteps of Essek William Kenyon (1867–1948). In his writings, Hagin copied word-for-word from Kenyon, while claiming to have been inspired by God.[367] And E. W. Kenyon was not rooted at all in the Holiness movement or Pentecostals but in what is called "metaphysics" in the United States,[368] which includes Christian Science, the New Thought movement, the Unity School of Christianity, and the Science of Mind. A man called John Kennington, which originally saw Kenyon as his spiritual father but whose teachings he gradually came to see as sectarian, is said to have reported the following: "What surprised me were the similarities between what he [Kenyon] conveyed and what Christian Science taught. We talked about these similarities, and he admitted them. I remember how he said, 'The only thing that Christian Science is missing is the blood of Christ.'" Purportedly, Kenyon was also quite closely acquainted with the writings of Ralph Waldo Emerson and the New England Transcendentalism, the forerunner of the New Thought movement. Much of this, by the way, goes back to Phineas P. Quimby (1802–1866), a para-psychologist who, in 1862, healed Mary Baker Eddy, the founder of Christian Science, and it seems that his teaching formed the basis for her cult of spiritual science.[370]

To demonstrate the basis for this teaching, I best refer to my own spiritual development, which started with Christian Science. The following is a text I wrote in 1996 to inform Charismatic Catholics who worked together with me for the kingdom of God:

"Freed from Esoteric Sect: Harald G. Huber's Life Story

There are many different forms of the esoteric. One of them is to equate our thinking with reality, that is, to think that our thinking can directly shape reality. It is a form of magic. I am able to talk about it because I grew up in a sect in which the goal was to apply this to our daily lifes, experiencing the effectiveness of this method. This was the sect of "Christian Science," founded by Mary Baker Eddy in the United States. Its headquarters are in Boston, but it has branches all over the world. For this sect, good and evil are mainly a mistake in our thinking, and it is enough to remove this mistaken thinking to turn the world into something effectively good.

Every Sunday, my mother went to the sect's local gathering, and I went to its "Sunday school" until I was twenty. There, I learned that our thinking was responsible for the negative things in the world and that correcting our thinking had a direct impact on our environment. I experienced how this worked when—which rarely happened—I was sick. My mother never contacted a doctor. Usually, she just ignored the fact that I was sick, or she might get a so-called "wielder" who took charge of my case, meaning to work on it mentally. Since I was never seriously sick, I cannot say what caused my recoveries.

In retrospect, I find that I was strangely immune against this teaching and practice, and I did things that did not at all fit in with it. When I was still in primary school, for instance, I had the idea of putting my toy stable under a Christmas tree, adding not only the animals but also Mary and the Christ child. Why did I have the urge to do this? Was it only a game? Today, I tend to see the influence of divine grace in this, protecting me.

Strangely enough, I cannot remember that my mother ever directly asked me to think something that was not in line with reality. Of course, she did it in more indirect ways, for example, by calling a sickness a "mistake." But she was not very insistent. Nor did I try very hard to put the theory I had learned into practice. Occasionally, when playing a game, I tried to influence the outcome of the dice with my mental power, which I did manage to do. But I did not do it frequently, and it definitely never became a compulsion on my part.

I am emphasizing how little I was influenced by the practice of Christian Science to make the point that, even with my rather slight entanglement in esoteric teachings, I later needed to go through an intense process of deliverance.

Actually, I was baptized as a Protestant and therefore a member of the Evangelic National Church. When I was sixteen, my Sunday-school teacher asked me if I wanted to become a member of Christian Science. This was unusual, since one usually had to be twenty to become a member of the local branch. But there was the possibility of becoming a member of the "mother church" in Boston when you were sixteen. Apparently, my answers in Sunday school gave the impression that I had a firm grasp on the teachings of the sect. But there was no question for me: I did not want to become a member.

In fact, I was ashamed to be in this sect. Although I did not attend either the optional Protestant or the Catholic religious education in school, I avoided giving a reason for my decision. Outside of "Sunday school," I did not talk with anyone about religious questions.

My problems seemed to lie elsewhere. I was only fifteen when I felt such despair about the question of the meaning of life that I seriously thought about ending my life. Outwardly, there was absolutely no reason for my depression. I was a successful student and got along well with my classmates. My home situation was normal. My problem was evidently more rooted in metaphysics, and it was no accident that I later studied Existential philosophy. In any case, Christian Science could not help me. What was the use of attaining health and well-being by the power of thought if life itself had no meaning anyway?

Again, it was the grace of God that came to my help. I had the thought: if I was willing to kill myself, then why not rather step back and watch my life as if observing it from the outside? From then on, suicide was not an issue anymore, but I was in a strange state of detachment—of solitude—from what was going on in the world. I purposefully use the word *seclusion* (Abgeschiedenheit), which I later met in the mystic Meister Eckhart. My life was now based on a spiritual element that usually only appears at a later stage: the night of the senses—and maybe also of the spirit. But untimely graces do not necessarily positive effect. To me, it felt like being a walking dead.

Even back then, I saw a connection between having grown up under the influence of Christian Science and my death wish. Somewhere, I heard that the suicide rate among children whose parents belonged to Christian Science was higher than average. This seems rather surprising, considering that they consider everything that is bad in the world as merely a mistake that may well be overlooked. Later, I realized that it was precisely this way of dealing with evil that caused it to reappear in more powerful and often nightmarish forms. I could name a few examples, such as unexplained appearances of cancer. In my view, there is such a thing as "esoteric cancer."

I cannot give a complete account of my further development here; some of it would be off-topic anyway. The main point is that, as a university student, I was in a deep crisis. In school, I had done just enough to get by. I did pay attention in class, but I only did my homework when it was absolutely necessary. Now, at university, I gave everything, pursuing two full study programs. In addition, I studied philosophy, particularly German Idealism (Kant, Schelling, Fichte, and Hegel). Gradually, I developed a neurosis that had possibly already started earlier. I did not sleep well and started to lose my memory, which made it increasingly difficult to learn. I lacked an inner calm and was less and less capable of relating to other people. My first clear outward failure came when I failed a final exam with a professor, forcing me to repeat it.

It was in this situation that I had a revelation about who Jesus Christ was. I read Hegel's *Philosophy of History* where it says, "World history moves to and from Jesus Christ." When I read this, the name of Jesus Christ seemed to light up, and everything else retired into the background. I immediately knew that Jesus Christ was something special. He was the source from which I could expect new life in my hopeless situation. He was the anchor I could hold on to.

Of course, I did more or less know the Bible. The liturgy of Christian Science consisted of reading carefully picked-out Bible verses together with passages from the teaching book of Mrs. Baker Eddy. Also, I had read in Hegel's *Philosophy of Religion* a number of things about the meaning of the death and resurrection of Jesus Christ, even if some of it was wrong and distorted. This amount of information, together with the blowing of the Holy Spirit, was enough to make me realize that my salvation came from the cross.

Interestingly, at the forefront of my concerns was not the question of sin and guilt but my sleep disorder. God used it to lead me to the faith. I saw that faith was much like falling asleep. It is impossible to fall asleep willfully, because the effort of the will only makes one more awake. In the same way, it is impossible to believe by an effort of the will, since faith is about submitting one's own will to the will of God. One has to leave one's spirit with Jesus Christ, allowing it to die with him. This is not easy, and it does require effort in the sense of focusing on God in meditation. But I made progress, and I received a new spirit, free of the sickness of my old self. Gradually, I learned to fall asleep again without a problem, by casting my sleeplessness on Jesus Christ who took it with him in his death on the cross. This helped me to realize later that the controversy between the Reformers and the Catholic Church regarding the nature of faith was a false dichotomy. The argument was about whether fiducial faith, that is, a general trust in God, was enough for salvation or whether one also needed a theological faith, that is, the faith that we were redeemed through the death and resurrection of Jesus Christ, the Son of God who had become flesh. Obviously, what is needed is both. We need a theological faith in the cross, for only when our faith is attached to the cross can it become what it needs to be, namely an activity of my thinking and willing as a prerequisite for a new birth of my human spirit from the Spirit of God. This kind of faith, however, is also always a fiducial faith.

What was important for me was to expect my salvation from the cross alone. I am grateful to God that I did not have to count many "sheep" to fall asleep, and that I never had to take any pills. And, even more, I am grateful that God protected me from seeking my salvation in non-Christian meditation or even drugs. Through my faith, I felt his grace flowing into my heart, allowing me to partake in the resurrection of Christ. I received the assurance that this truly was my salvation, the beginning of a new life that would never end.

This was different from what Christian Science tried to offer, and I experienced everything that came from that direction as something that tried to hinder me on my new path. It was a thick fog that threatened to block out the sun. How often did I pray, "Lord Jesus Christ, don't let me perish!" I went down into the basement or outside in the forest and prayed loudly. I also formulated a renunciation of Christian Science, similar to the liturgy of baptism in which one renounces the Devil. In the forest, I also burned the teaching book of Christian Science that my mother had given me. It was a thick volume that did not burn easily.

In those days, I did a number of things that might be seen as extreme, among them my loud praying, which eventually led to praying in tongues. I immediately knew what was happening, as I had read First Corinthians. Later, when my spiritual situation stabilized, I gave up my loud praying, including praying in tongues. It took twenty years for me to get to know the Charismatic Renewal. It was then that I remembered that I used to pray in tongues, and I was immediately able to do it again.

My renunciation of Christian Science was not enough. I felt that there was an actual spiritual war, and I commanded these powers in the name of Jesus Christ to leave me. My change put a large strain on my relationship with my mother. She suffered from a heart condition but hid this fact, hoping to experience healing through Christian Science. Finally, when her condition was so serious that there was no more avoiding a doctor, it was already too late. I committed her spirit to the redemptive death of Jesus Christ, in the hope that she would be touched by him. Shortly after, she died. It was a Good Friday. Those who die with Christ will also be raised with him.

But I was only completely freed from the evil spirit of Christian Science when I started to go on the offensive. I proclaimed the power of Christ over these people and seriously considered going to one of their meetings and giving testimony about the power of Christ's blood. I ended up not doing it, though.

By opening myself up to Jesus Christ and being freed from the dark powers of Christian Science, God's grace was increasingly poured into my heart. In the beginning, I kept having moments in which great joy and warmth overcame me, and it was as if prayers poured out of me by themselves. My indifference toward the world, which had been my companion for quite some time, now turned into the ability to find joy independently from the world. And instead of my lacking relationships, I was now happy to approach others and have fellowship with them. I also became freer on the inside. My neurosis disappeared quite quickly and my intellectual faculties returned. I completed my second degree with distinction. Soon, I was filled by something that I experienced as both warm and cold: warm in that it gave me a sense of security, and cold in that it made me free.

Christian Science is clearly a non-Christian sect. For them, the world as such is good, and evil only springs from our wrong thinking that needs to be corrected. Hence, redemption through the Son of God is unnecessary. The word *science* actually denotes the empirical natural sciences. Christian Science sees the death and resurrection of Jesus Christ simply as evidence that death is only an error in our thinking. An ideology such as Christian Science is not simply false and ineffective but is connected to ancient forms of magic in which man visualized concrete goals and focused all the power of his thoughts on actually experiencing the visualized goal. This was how the prehistorical hunting magic worked, and this is how other practices work, from Eastern religions to the method of a basketball player in visualizing the ball being in the net before throwing it.

This seems to be what was meant in the first of the Ten Commandments where it says, "You shall not carve idols for yourselves in the shape of anything in the sky above or on the earth below or in the waters beneath the earth; you shall not bow down before them or worship them." When we read this, we usually think of images of gods, but it applies just as much to the technique of magic. After all, one of the meanings of worship is: to think something true. In antiquity, Egypt was known for its magic, and it was Egypt that the Israelites—and we!—were to leave.

In the Old Testament, it is often emphasized that idols are only stone and wood, void of any power. The commandment not to worship them seems like nothing more than jealousy on the part of God. But the Apostle Paul explains why God is "jealous" for our sakes. He says that behind the objects being worshipped there are demons that are eager to be worshipped and receive some of the worship given to the idols. This, of course, is also true of thoughts and ideas that we worship as supposed reality.

This means that systems of thought such as Christian Science call on demons, and this is where they receive their power. However, demons always demand a price, namely the soul of the person who gets involved with them. They start to have power over the person, and he can only get free through the blood of Christ.

Often, the true faith lies right next to the abyss of the occult, and it requires a high degree of discernment to point to the right way. As is well known, there is a saying of Jesus in the Gospel of Mark that says, "Therefore I tell you, whatever you ask for in prayer, believe that you have received it, and it will be yours" (Mk 11:24; NIV). Within Evangelical-Pentecostal circles, this verse is taken as the basis for a school of thought that is known as "Word of Faith." Adherents include people such as Kenneth Hagin, John Osteen, Kenneth Copeland, K.C. Price, T.L. Osborn, and Don Gosset—and, according to some, also Agnes Sanford und Yonggi Cho. They teach that prayer is supposed to be very specific: that one needs to visualize what one prays for and should proclaim that it has already been fulfilled. They also teach that God does not only want to heal people through such prayer but also make them prosperous.

Recent research has shown that these teachings did not grow out of the womb of Pentecostalism but rather of Christian Science. It was E.W. Kenyon who, as it were, baptized the teachings of Christian Science (as well as related ideas such as the "Unity" and the "New Thought" movements) and gave them a Christian mold. It was from him that Kenneth Hagin, a Pentecostal from Texas, adopted these thoughts, and Hagin in turn became the father of the "Word of Faith" movement. Hagin, however, is a rather enigmatic personality. Today, we know that he actually plagiarized Kenyon, even though he always denied having been influenced by him, instead claiming to have received special revelations of Jesus Christ. The proclamation of this teaching was accompanied by strange threats against those who would not believe it. A number of people who, based on the Gospels, voiced doubts about the teaching, fell to the floor, unable to move until they pledged themselves to these teachings. Such things usually only occur in the occult. One should add, though, that there is no indication that similar things happened among other proponents of the Word of Faith movement.

Within Charismatic Catholicism, the Word of Fait h teaching was never a topic. This had different reasons. One of them is that the Catholic Church pre-empts the true part of the movement through its doctrine of the sacraments, and it does so in a way that is in line with the gospel. The first epistle of John also retains the word of Jesus that we find in Mark, but it is more elaborated (1Joh 14f.). According to this passage, it is only when we pray in accordance with God's will that we receive what we pray for. The seven sacraments in the Catholic Church are all in accordance with what Jesus Christ promised. This is what is meant when it is taught that the sacraments were instituted by Jesus.

As an infant, I was baptized by a Protestant minister, which is why all churches that believe in infant baptism do not tire of proclaiming that, by faith in the death and resurrection of Jesus Christ, God's Son who became flesh, I have died with him and been born again. They kept proclaiming this for twenty-five years, until I actually believed it, and, to my delight, it became a reality for me. And it would have been a violation of the faith to let myself be baptized again.

The Catholic idea of the sacraments has nothing to do with magic. Rather, it lays claim on what has been promised. As a rule, this is something that the proponents of the Word of Faith movement overlook. Usually, what happens is that they more or less silently assume that what they lay claim to is a general or individual promise of God. Even Hagin teaches that our claims are based on God's promises, but he does not look seriously into what these promises are, or he presupposes promises that are no such thing.

The basis for a claim is not only a universal promise of God but also, for instance, a "word of knowledge," meaning a specific Charismatic word directed at a specific person or group of persons. Such a word of knowledge, too, may and should be claimed as something that has already happened. In contrast, the promises that are underlying the sacraments are never very specific. The anointing of the sick, for instance, might bring about healing, but it might also bring about a good death or the ability to bear the sickness. Charismatic words, in contrast, are tailored to the specific needs of individuals.

Literature by/about the Word of Faith Movement:

Hagin, Kenneth: *The Art of Prayer*
Farah, Charles: *From the Pinnacle of the Temple*
Cornwall, Judson: *It's God's War: A Biblical View of Spiritual Warfare*
Wilkerson, David: *Set the Trumpet to Thy Mouth*
McConnell, D.R.: *A Different Gospel"*

From my current perspective, I would like to add the following to what I wrote before: (1) It seems that, in the United States, there were also Catholic Charismatics who invited Kenneth Hagin to speak. (2) The spread of Christian Science seems to have been reduced greatly everywhere. As far as Switzerland is concerned, I know this from personal experience. On the other hand, there is still a disciple of Hagin in Switzerland who has a relatively large congregation and a strong platform on the radio and the internet.

There are two aspects of the teachings of the Word of Faith movement that are worth highlighting: One is the way the nature of faith is viewed, and the other one is the very worldly effects and goals of faith, namely health, wealth, and success.

A. The view on faith: Knowledge differentiated between knowledge of the senses (the empirical sciences) and knowledge of revelation.[371] The latter is about the supernatural knowledge of God and the spiritual kingdom as revealed in the Bible. Kenyon teaches that knowledge of the senses should be denied. It is the human spirit, not the body or soul, that possesses the knowledge of revelation. Hagin says that "one almost has to by-pass the brain and operate from the inner man (the heart or spirit) to really get into the things of God."[372] Everything perceived by the senses has to be denied. This reminds me of M.B. Eddy who calls such perception an "error." Of course, it would be a true teaching to say that we can have a relationship with God through our heart. But the Word of Faith movement takes this into a completely different direction than

Christianity. The relationship with God is practically non-existent. Knowledge of the spirit is knowledge of the sensible world. Faith does not relate to a loving God and even less to the Son. About him, it is taught that he does not suffer primarily on the cross but at the hands of the Devil in the underworld. Nor is it necessary to be led by the Holy Spirit. As Hagin writes: "Did you ever stop to think about having faith in your faith? Evidently God had faith in His faith, because He spoke words of faith and they came to pass. … In other words, having faith in your words is having faith in your faith. That's what you've got to learn to do to get things from God: Have faith in your faith" (*Having Faith in Your Faith*, p. 4-5). Further, he taught that God was not a Person but a mental principle. Even those who do not believe in him can make use of the teaching of faith. Faith, being independent of the will of God, needs to be made effective through confession. We speak, and it comes to pass. Man, made in the image of God, can be just as creative as God himself. Says Hagin, "Have the faith of God,"[374] by which he does not mean faith *in* God. Those who are born again are not just the body of Christ but a god like Christ.[375]

B. Sickness: According to the Word of Faith teaching, sickness is a spiritual condition that shows itself in the body.[376] This means healing has to be spiritual, too.[377] A true Christian is never sick. Sickness has been laid on Jesus. Sickness is always caused by unbelief and sin. Symptoms of disease are to be denied and should not be mentioned. Medical care is to be rejected. Believers should not die due to sickness;[378] and never before they reach seventy years. Actually, one should reach 120, as promised in the Bible.[379]

C. Prosperity:[380] Hagin teaches: "He [God] wants His children to eat the best, He wants them wear the best clothing, He wants them to drive the best cars, and He wants them to have the best of everything."[381] There is no difference between the basic needs of a believer and his fleshly desires.

D. True Christian teaching: In opposition of the Word of Faith teaching, one needs to quote the Bible, particularly Paul: "Therefore, we are not discouraged; rather, although our outer self is wasting away, our inner self is being renewed day by day. For this momentary light affliction is producing for us an eternal weight of glory beyond all comparison, as we look not to what is seen but to what is unseen; for what is seen is transitory, but what is unseen is eternal."[382] But much more extreme is what Paul writes about himself later in same letter: "I know someone in Christ who, fourteen years ago … was caught up to the third heaven. And I know that this person … was caught up into Paradise and heard ineffable things, which no one may utter. … Therefore, that I might not become too elated, a thorn in the flesh was given to me, an angel of Satan, to beat me, to keep me from being too elated. Three times I begged the Lord about this, that it might leave me, but he said to me, 'My grace is sufficient for you, for power is made perfect in weakness.'" Before this passage, Paul again listed the things he suffered for Christ.[384] Calling it a small burden is obviously an understatement. The fact is that the Christian life consists of two things: suffering in this world and a view of the glory of God. This can be more or less intense. Christians take part in the cross of Christ but also in his resurrection. As the Lord says, "Whoever wishes to come after me must deny himself, take up his cross, and follow me."[385] And: "Whoever loses his life for my sake will find it."[386] In the most extreme case, a Christian becomes a martyr and actually sees the heavens open, as in the case of Stephen when he was stoned.[387] The connection to heaven is not always equally strong, but it can be strengthened through various spiritual disciplines. On the most basic level, one can say like the disciples on the way to Emmaus, "Were not our hearts burning?"[388] Part of this is connection is built through prayer, particularly the praying in tongues of Pentecostals as well as "resting in the Spirit" as a result of a blessing, but also the Eucharist of Catholics, as they believe—and this becomes a reality for them—that Jesus' charge "Do this in remembrance of me" does not only refer to the eating of food but also to his words "This is my body" and "This is my blood," thus changing both into the body and blood of Christ, allowing the believer to maintain a direct bond to the divinity of Christ. Through this burning in our hearts, our sufferings in the world become insignificant and life gains meaning, making it unnecessary to find meaning in drugs. Also, the soul is sanctified and freed of the consequences of sin.

Particularly in countries in which Pentecostalism is persecuted, it is receiving this grace, developing primarily through speaking in tongues and often also resting in the Spirit.[389] Due to the deliverance that faith in the death and resurrection of Jesus Christ brings, one can open oneself up to the grace of such a mystical relationship with God, making it possible to say together with Paul, "It is no longer I who live, but Jesus Christ who lives in me." Being filled on the inside in such a way, it becomes the foundation for becoming active in love: praying for others, engaging in missions and charity. Christ always remains the gate to this kind of mysticism, which means that there is no entry for evil spirits.

As far as the desire for worldly riches is concerned, the chapter on poverty should have already clarified quite a bit. We can also quote the first epistle of John: "Do not love the world or the things of the world. If anyone loves the world, the love of the Father is not in him. For all that is in the world, sensual lust, enticement for the eyes, and a pretentious life, is not from the Father but is from the world."[390]

The conclusion is that the teaching on faith and prosperity is not biblically founded. One is reminded of Paul's remark about people who teach wrong things: that they do go to heaven "but only as through fire."[391] It could also be that these teachings are so far removed from the truth and a relationship with God and, most importantly, are not built on the foundation of Jesus Christ that heaven remains closed to these people. When I started to cut my ties to Christian Science, I still felt burdened by evil spirits for a considerable period of time. I would also like to refer to Jesus' words to the Laodicean church in Revelation: "… because you are lukewarm, neither hot nor cold, I will spit you out of my mouth. For you say, 'I am rich and affluent and have no need of anything,' and yet do not realize that you are wretched, pitiable, poor, blind, and naked. I advise you to buy from me … ointment to smear on your eyes so that you may see."[392] This "seeing" does not only mean seeing one's own condition but also seeing into the kingdom of heaven.

I would like to round off these remarks about the true content of the Christian faith by pointing to what Jesus Christ himself has taught. It was in accordance with the will of his heavenly Father that he allowed himself to be crucified, rising on the third day. And Jesus emphasizes that doing the will of the Father is his spiritual food.[393] Finally, he calls us to take up our cross and follow him.[394] Carrying his cross is something that first has to happen on the inside, separating oneself from the world, as Paul indicated, and reaching out to the kingdom of heaven. From there, we receive blessed nourishment, just like Jesus did. This is known as asceticism and mysticism, and it is promoted by Holy Communion as well as the Baptism with the Holy Spirit and speaking in tongues. But it also happens outwardly when we suffer or even die for our faith. As already mentioned, it was in such a moment that Stephen saw the heavens open and was nourished from above. "But he, filled with the holy Spirit, looked up intently to heaven and saw the glory of God and Jesus standing at the right hand of God ..."[395] This is happening again to a high degree. The time of the Antichrist[396] is transitioning to the time of the Tribulation, and Christians are being attacked by terrorists. But, once again, Satan will have the opposite effect of what he intends: the cross of Christ will become real to people and many will come to believe and soon be unified with the Lord. Jesus did not only call believers to take up their cross but also lightened their burden in this world. He healed them, delivered them from demons, and gave them grace in different ways. Yet not without a reason: he wanted to lead people to the faith so that they would experience his love even more powerfully in heaven.[397] It is not without reason that it is mostly missionaries who demonstrate many visible healings at large evangelistic meetings, causing people to give their lives to Christ.

Chapter 9

The Charismatic Renewal

A. General Remarks

In the 1950s, the so-called Second Wave of the Holy Spirit began. The Pentecostal movement spilled over into traditional denominations. This mainly came to be known as the "Charismatic Renewal." It is important, however, to distinguish the situation among the Reformed churches from that within Catholicism. Among Reformed Christians, the predominant view was that the charismata had ceased after the apostolic age. This is why the gifts of the Spirit met with virulent rejection at first. In the Catholic Church, on the other hand, the gifts of the Spirit were never rejected in principle. In fact, it was and still is true that no one can be considered a saint without having worked at least two well-attested miracles. Admittedly, in the Second Vatican Council there was at first the view that miracles only happened by way of exception (Cardinal Ruffini of Palermo), a view which Cardinal Suenens vehemently contradicted, causing the Council to adopt a resolution more in favor of miracles.[398] This does not preclude that there are still Catholics today who think that miracles are extremely exceptional occurrences. One problem that still exists in the Catholic Church is the teaching of the sacraments, of which four can only be administered by an ordained priest or bishop (the Eucharist, Confirmation, Anointing of the Sick, and Absolution on the basis of Confession). In spite of the Council decision to the contrary, it is still seen by many as a great exception for the Holy Spirit to work miracles through ordinary believers. At the most, people expect miracles in special places in which the Virgin Mary is venerated, such as Lourdes, and then usually only during the Blessed Sacrament of the Eucharist when the bread is changed. In contrast to this, church history teaches that, over and over, miracles have happened in answer to the prayer of believing Catholics. Don Bosco, for instance, was surrounded on his journey to France because of miracles.

Anglicans—known outside of England as "Episcopals"—take a middle ground between Reformed and Catholics.

To go more into detail, the Charismatic Renewal developed as follows:[399] Before the Renewal, Pentecostals were outcasts. Most of them were poor, underprivileged, uneducated, and out of touch with the trends of Modernism and the Social Gospel within mainline Protestantism. On the part of Protestants, they were generally despised, relegated to the ranks of the poor and outsiders who were not welcome in the increasingly rich and intellectual mainline churches.

Both Protestants and Catholics were unaware of the exponential growth of the Pentecostal movement in the first half of the twentieth century. Speaking in tongues, prophecy and exorcism were seen as bizarre byproducts of religious intolerance. Healing, meanwhile, pulled a considerable number into Pentecostal congregations, which led to splits among friends and families.

After the Second World War, Pentecostalism grew to such an extent that it could no longer be ignored. Pentecostals began to erect large, modern church buildings that were quite noticeable. In addition, there were Pentecostal services on TV. Healings happened in people's living rooms. Particularly Catholics were attracted.

Before 1960, pastors who spoke in tongues were generally banned from their church, which caused many to either switch over to the Pentecostals or to keep it a secret. Laypersons, too, switched over to Pentecostal congregations, not least because they found the worship, miracles, singing, clapping and dancing before the Lord in the services there attractive.

The first breakthrough came in November 1950 with the Episcopal pastor Dennis Bennet in California. He experienced speaking in tongues after friends had prayed for him, which forced him to resign from his church. His resolute testimony caused a major media stir, leading him to be active in Seattle, Washington, for twenty years, gathering supporters. A whole avalanche of pastors and laypeople followed him, among them Larry Christenson (Lutheran), James Browns (Presbyterian), Howard

Conatser (Southern Baptist), and Nelson Litwiller (Mennonite). It was the start of the Charismatic Renewal within Protestant denominations. In 1956, the Episcopal priest Richard Winkler, leader of the Trinity Episcopal Church in Wheaton, Illinois, received the gift of tongues. As a result, he conducted healing services in his church during which many members had Pentecostal experiences.

That the first breakthroughs happened among Episcopals is not surprising, since, as already mentioned, they take a middle ground between Protestantism and Catholicism.

Among Lutherans, the Charismatic breakthrough was more problematic. Apart from the early Lutheran Charismatic Harald Bredesen, who joined the Assemblies of God already in 1947,[400] Larry Christenson was the main initiator of the Charismatic Renewal among Lutherans. Luther had not only opposed the peasant revolts and the Anabaptists but had also been rather antagonistic toward miracles, which he viewed as Roman-Catholic superstitions.[401] I have already mentioned that he rejected healing.[402] In the end, however, the renewal of the Spirit was theologically more or less accepted among Lutherans,[403] making it possible for the movement to spread worldwide.

Among Scottish Presbyterians and Swiss Reformed, Calvin (besides Zwingli) was the main foundation. He did not reject the gifts of the Spirit *per se* but thought that they had ceased because of a lack of faith.[404] He did not see them as condemnable, then. On the contrary, they played a significant role in his theology of the Holy Spirit. In contrast to Luther, he also taught that justification through faith in Jesus Christ brings with it sanctification.[405] In spite of this, the majority of Calvinists later rejected miracles after the time of the Apostles.[406] When, after the Second World War, the Charismatic Renewal started in the mainline denominations in the United States, it was James Brown near Philadelphia whose experience of the Baptism in the Holy Spirit with accompanying speaking in tongues caused him to change from an extremely liberal theological position to a Charismatic Evangelical stance.[407] At first, he thought he would have to leave the Presbyterian church, and he asked the famous Pentecostal leader David du Plessis for advice, who replied, “Stay in your church and renew it.” Brown followed this advice, leaving the Presbyterian Sunday services the way they were but, in addition, holding Charismatic services on Saturday night. This worked for twenty years with minimal friction. Later, when Dennis Bennett became the leading Charismatic Presbyterian, Pentecostalism gained wider visibility and more frictions arose. A significant role was played by the former jurist Brick Bradford who founded the "Presbyterian Charismatic Communion" (PCC) in 1968.

There were additional Charismatic Renewal movements among specifically American denominations, such as among Methodists, Baptists, and Mennonites, but also reaching as far as the Orthodox and finally the United Church of Christ, a church that partly goes back to the Puritan Pilgrims who arrived in America in the 1620s.

The Catholic Peter Hocken, in the *New International Dictionary of Pentecostal and Charismatic Movements*, by Burgess and Van der Maas, has written extensively about the Charismatic Renewal.[408] According to him, the Charismatic Renewal has nine characteristics:[409]

Focus on Jesus

The focus is on a close relationship with him and the acknowledgement of him as Lord. In this connection, I again want to point out that the outpouring of the Holy Spirit has a close affinity to the devotion to the Sacred Heart of Jesus.

Worship

The Spirit leads to the worship of God the Father and the Son. Never before in the history of Christianity have so many songs been written (cf. Joh 7:38).

Love for the Bible

Hocken avoids calling it Evangelicalism.

God is Still Speaking Today

What believers hear from God is in addition to the Bible. What is essential is God's relationship with his "children." The main thing is the revelation about who Christ is (Joh 16:13-15).

Evangelism

The Spirit gives believers an evangelistic mindset from within and helps them from without to have the means for evangelism.

Acknowledgement of the Devil

In particular, exorcism is practiced as well.

Spiritual Gifts

First Corinthians 12:8-10: speaking in tongues, prophecy, and healing.

Eschatological Expectation

The second coming of Christ. "Come, Lord Jesus."

Spiritual Power

The powerless church will receive new power.

The fact is that Pentecostals and Charismatics agree on these nine points.

The differences lie elsewhere.[410] In the First World, Charismatics are mostly white people from middle-class backgrounds. Pentecostals, on the other hand, are proletarians of all colors. In the Third World, however, particularly in Asia, the Charismatic movement has made great strides since the 1970s.

Among different Charismatics, the way believers were led to the Baptism in the Spirit was very different.

At least in the beginning, the mission of Charismatics was not so much directed at unbelievers as at the members of their own denominations. Even in 2001, I was still part of a Catholic Charismatic community in which evangelism had this direction, not least because it is undeniable that many members in the mainline denominations are not actually believers.

Among Pentecostals, the main concern is sanctification, both on the inside and through good works. Among Charismatics, the focus tends to be more on the community of the church.

Pentecostals tend to adhere to premillennialism, that is, the peculiar teaching of the "rapture" at the second coming of Christ, as well as to dispensationalism, which was invented by Scofield, publicized in his annotated Bible shortly after the birth of the Pentecostal movement. Originally, the teaching was meant to show why there were no more miracles, but Pentecostals reinterpreted it and used it, among other things, to substantiate their premillennialism.[411] In his work *The Century of the Holy Spirit*, Synan deals neither with premillennialism nor dispensationalism, ignoring their theories on the rapture.[412] It seems as though these teachings are no longer universally advocated even among Pentecostals.

Nor is the ministry of healing the same everywhere. Among Pentecostals, it is more focused on outward healing; among Charismatics, more on inward healing. This has to do both with social and theological differences.

Charismatics have repeatedly worked through the experience of the Baptism in the Holy Spirit theologically. Among Pentecostals, the Baptism in the Holy Spirit and speaking in tongues belong together. Among Charismatics, this is not necessarily the case.

Often, Charismatics only pray for the Holy Spirit, forgetting the cross, which is the foundation. The "Life in the Spirit" seminar that has its origins in Ann Arbor, Michigan, and is often used by Catholics does not emphasize the cross at all.[413] This is why I have always used the seminar by Pater Ernst Sievers instead, which is better.[414] It is encouraging that the new German edition of "Life in the Spirit" has adopted several aspects of the seminar by Sievers, and it is now called *"Leben aus der Kraft des Heiligen Geistes"* ("Life in the Power of the Spirit").[415]

Following the Charismatic Renewal, there is the "Third Wave," which can take quite different forms and is quantitatively much more extensive, particularly in the Third World.[416]

B. The Charismatic Renewal in the Catholic Church

The Charismatic development within the Catholic Church is unique for several reasons. For one, the Catholic Church never rejected signs and wonders and has always emphasized the inner sanctification that comes through faith. There was also definite inspiration about strengthening the charismata, particularly coming from the papacy. Already during the Council of Trient following the Reformation (1545–1563), the state of affairs in the Catholic Church was strongly criticized. That is the reason it is often called the "Counter Reformation," not because it was about winning Protestants back to Catholicism, though that was certainly an issue as well. Further, as I have already set forth in Chapter V, Sister Elena Guerra caused Pope Leo XIII (1878–1903) to publish in 1895 the call to prayer for the Holy Spirit, followed in 1897 by the encyclical *Divinum illud munus* about the Holy Spirit. And, finally, on January 1, 1901, he consecrated the world to the Holy Spirit. In the encyclical, we find the remark that there are people (Catholics) who do not even know that there is a Holy Spirit. I have experienced this myself in 1997. I was part of a Charismatic community in Hamburg, and we had a daily prayer meeting. One of the attendees was an old German woman from Upper Silesia (Poland). Somehow the topic of the Trinity came up in our conversation, and she remarked, "It's quite simple—it's like a family: a Father, a Mother, and a Son." She did not respond to my objection. Apparently, this is what she had learned in her youth.

The activities of Pope Leo XIII had almost no consequences in the Catholic Church. Instead, January 1, 1901, was the date when the Pentecostal movement was born. Some people compare this to the situation in the early church where, though Jesus Christ proclaimed the gospel primarily to Jews, it was mostly the Gentiles who received it, and it is only at the end of time that the Israelites will be grafted back into it. The next initiative regarding the charismata in the Catholic Church came from Pope John XXIII (1958–1963). Apparently, he already had some Charismatic experiences before he became pope. As Bishop Angelo Roncalli, he regularly visited a small Czechoslovakian village of about three-hundred people where, for many centuries, Catholics had been experiencing all the spiritual gifts listed in First Corinthians 12. It was just part of their normal Christian life.[417] Patti Gallagher Mansfield learned of this through her friend Anna-Mariae Schmidt who is from that village and was there when Angelo Roncalli came to visit. She tells the story of how, in the eleventh century, frost destroyed the grain on their fields and the villagers feared to die of hunger, but then, as they prayed for help, a beautiful woman appeared and taught them to call on the Holy Spirit. This led the villagers to experience the blessings of the Spirit in more concrete ways. The village recovered from the famine and started living a life marked by Christian love—for centuries. In the 1930s, then, there was a prophecy that the village would have to endure a severe trial. Shortly after, in 1938, Nazis invaded the village, killing almost everyone. Anna-Mariae Schmidt survived and spent time in concentration camps, first under the Nazis, then the Russians.

Elena Guerra was the first person whom Pope John XXIII beatified, calling her the "Apostle of the Holy Spirit." And, at the start of the Second Vatican Council, he said the following prayer: "Renew your wonders in our time, as though for a new Pentecost, and grant that the holy Church, preserving unanimous and continuous prayer, together with Mary, the mother of Jesus, and also under the guidance of St. Peter, may increase the reign of the Divine Savior, the reign of truth and justice, the reign of love and peace. Amen." On January 1, 1959, Pope John XXIII announced the Second Vatican Council, which was opened on October 11, 1962 and lasted until December 8, 1965. On September 7, 1965, the *Lumen Gentium* (the Dogmatic Constitution of the Church) was proclaimed,[418] which includes the following text:

"It is not only through the sacraments and the ministries of the Church that the Holy Spirit sanctifies and leads the people of God and enriches it with virtues, but, 'allotting his gifts to everyone according as He wills' (1Cor 12:11). He distributes special graces among the faithful of every rank. By these gifts He makes them fit and ready to undertake the various tasks and offices which contribute toward the renewal and building up of the Church, according to the words of the Apostle: 'The manifestation of the Spirit is given to everyone for profit' (1Cor 12:7). These charisms, whether they be the more outstanding or the more simple and widely diffused, are to be received with thanksgiving and consolation for they are perfectly suited to and useful for the needs of the Church. Extraordinary gifts are not to be sought after, nor are the fruits of apostolic labor to be presumptuously expected from their use; but judgment as to their genuinity and proper use belongs to those who are appointed leaders in the Church, to whose special competence it belongs, not indeed to extinguish the Spirit, but to test all things and hold fast to that which is good (cf. 1Thess 5:12; 19-21)."

It is interesting that this text cites First Corinthians 12 where the supernatural gifts of the Spirit are mentioned. Usually, it is only the seven gifts listed in Isaiah that are referred to, which are basically just natural gifts that are strengthened.[419]

Even before the Council, David du Plessis—nicknamed "Mr. Pentecost"—had established a connection between the Pentecostal movement and the Catholic Church. This Pentecostal had an important mission from God, which Smith Wigglesworth passed on to him in a prophetic word from God in 1936:[420] "I have been sent by the Lord to tell you what he has shown me this morning. Through the old-line denominations will come a revival that will eclipse anything we have known throughout history. No such things have happened in times past as will happen when this begins. It will eclipse the present-day, twentieth-century Pentecostal revival that already is a marvel to the world, with its strong opposition from the established church. But the same blessing will become acceptable to the churches and they will go on with this message and this experience beyond what the Pentecostals have achieved. You will live to see this work grow to such dimensions that the Pentecostal movement itself will be a light thing in comparison with what God will do through the old churches. There will be tremendous gatherings of people, unlike anything we've seen, and great leaders will change their attitudes and accept not only the message but also the blessing."—"The Lord said to me that I am to give you warning that He is going to use you in this movement. You will have a very prominent part.'"[420] To Pentecostal ears, this was unheard-of. Pentecostals always thought they had to distance themselves from the traditional churches. Finally, Wigglesworth told du Plessis that he only needed to start thinking about this prediction after he, Wigglesworth, was dead.[421] After that, he gave him a final word from the Lord: "If you remain humble and faithful, you will live to see the whole fulfilled."

Here, I will skip du Plessis' activities within Pentecostalism and Protestant churches, instead focusing on his not inconsiderable contact with the Catholic Church.[422]

Around 1960, Du Plessis was commissioned to speak during a meeting of the World Council of Churches in Scotland. He concluded his presentation with the following remark, "I am not here to confront you with Pentecostalism. I am here to defend it. I am here to confront you with Jesus Christ, who is the light of the world, but also the baptizer in the Holy Spirit. As far as I can see, Jesus never transferred this ministry to the church. It is a ministry that he has reserved for himself."

Hearing this, a man with a round white collar stepped up to him and said, "Allow a Catholic priest to thank you from the bottom of my heart for having drawn our attention to this Baptism in the Holy Spirit! I have always believed that I have the Holy Spirit. But tonight you have convinced me that I lack this Baptism."

As it turned out, this priest was an Oxford Professor (Bernhard Leeming) and a personal representative of Pope John. And he desired to receive the Baptism in the Holy Spirit from du Plessis. He, however, denied him this request, saying that you could only receive this Baptism from Jesus Christ directly. Leeming was astonished and impressed. Rome and the pope should hear this too, he said. After some inner hesitation, du Plessis agreed to come to Rome. In Rome (1961), then, he visited the office of Thomas Stransky, rector of the secretary of the Secretariat for the Promotion of Christian Unity, which, at the time, was led by Cardinal Bea. The office was full of books about Pentecostalism. Du Plessis asked about the books, to which Stransky explained, "The Holy Father said the prerequisite for a renewal of the church was a new Pentecost. We have been instructed to read everything about the Holy Spirit, and particularly about Pentecostals, that we can get our hands on." He wanted to talk to du Plessis because he had been informed by the World Council of Churches in Geneva that du Plessis was the only Pentecostal who was in dialogue with people outside of the Pentecostal movement, particularly with Catholics. What followed was a long and detailed conversation. Immediately after, du Plessis was received by Cardinal Bea, a German Jesuit who, against usual custom, was made bishop and cardinal by Pope John. Right away, they established friendly contact. In view of the upcoming Council, the cardinal asked, "What do the Pentecostals want to say to Rome?" Du Plessis' answer was: „Make the Bible available to every Catholic in the world in his own language.

The Holy Spirit will make that book come alive and that will change lifes and renew the church." Cardinal Bea stared at him, arose and exclaimed, "That is exactly what the Holy Father wants to know!"

Du Plessis was invited as a guest to the Council from 1962 to 1965. In 1963, Pope John was followed by Pope Paul VI.

From February 17 to 19, 1967, the "Duquesne Weekend" took place, which is generally seen as the beginning of the Charismatic Renewal in the Catholic Church. It was seventy years after the encyclical *Divinum illud munus* (about the Holy Spirit) by Pope Leo XIII.[423] And the full name of the Duquesne University in Pittsburg is "Duquesne University of the Holy Spirit," and on its emblem it says, *"Spiritus Est Qui Vivicat."* The university is led by the Holy Ghost Fathers, a missionary order.[424] At the university, there was also a prayer community (Chi Rho), although they were not particularly focused on the Spirit. Incidentally, the Duquesne University had connections to the University of Notre Dame in South Bend, Indiana.[425] There, the "Cursillo" became active, having a similar orientation. There were students who changed from one university to the other, building a network of friendships between the two places.[426]

On the weekend in question, twenty-five members of Chi Rho went to the retreat house "The Ark and the Dove" close to the university.[427] Leading the group were professors who had experienced the Baptism with the Holy Spirit a few weeks before[428] and who now read the first four chapters of Acts to the group, recommending that the students also read David Wilkerson's book *The Cross and the Switchblade*.[429] Another recommended book was *They Speak in Other Tongues* by John Sherrill.[430]

Friday night, there was a time for repentance.[431] On Saturday, they did not only hear a talk about Acts 2 but were also invited to receive both the Holy Spirit and Jesus,[432] making clear that people needed to give their lifes to Christ.[433] This led the participants to ask if they, who were baptized, had already received the Holy Spirit or not. David du Plessis, after all, had taught that the Baptism with the Holy Spirit did not take place through the laying on of hands in prayer but always had to be given by Jesus Christ directly.[434] The Catholics now reached the conclusion that they had to renew their baptism and Confirmation, in order to renew their relationship with Jesus Christ and be ready to be filled with the Holy Spirit.

For Saturday night, the original plan was a birthday party, which, though, did not really get going, in part because the running water in the house switched off and the house management asked the guests to return home. This caused some of them to go to the chapel and pray for the water to return, which did actually happen. Others joined them in the chapel and prayed before the changed bread of the Blessed Sacrament. There, they had a strong experience with the Lord, giving him their lifes and receiving the Baptism with the Holy Spirit, which included resting in the Spirit and other manifestations.

As explained earlier, the devotion to the Sacred of Jesus laid the foundation for precisely this kind of giving one's heart to Christ.[435]

Patti Gallagher Mansfield tells in detail how she experienced the Baptism with the Holy Spirit. She starts with the time of repentance on Friday night and what it meant for the Chi Rho members[436] who, in spite of their piousness, also had a tendency toward arguing, judging and grumbling. The Holy Spirit was visibly at work during this meeting, convicting all of their sins. Also, before every talk, they sang the song *Veni Creator Spiritus* in English, using a Gregorian melody. One of the leaders pointed out that this was actually a prayer.[437] Patti Gallagher Mansfield realized that the prayer she used to say, which basically amounted to "Lord, bless my plans; please do my will!", was not quite right. She had to repent and submit her free will to God, allowing him to be Lord and Master over everything. The leader asked her, "Are you ready for what the Holy Spirit wants to do in you?" She replied, "I'm afraid—afraid to be a fool."[438] Still, she was ready. When she knelt in the chapel in the Blessed Sacrament, she suddenly felt the presence of the Lord. Her body began to shake. She started being afraid of the greatness of God, and she told herself, "You had better get out of here quick before something happens to you." But overriding her fear was a much greater desire to surrender herself to God. She prayed, "Father, I give my life to you. Whatever you ask of me, I accept. And if it means suffering, I accept that too. Just teach me to follow Jesus and to love as he loves." In the next moment, she found herself prostrated, "resting in the Spirit." She was happy, having been baptized in the Holy Spirit.

At this point, I would like to say something about the dialectic of the relationship to God: When people submit their will to God, Jesus Christ is born spiritually in them and fills them with the Holy Spirit. This gives them a new freedom, because God is the Creator, and as such, he knows better what people really want than they know it themselves. In line with that, it says in Second Corinthians 3:17, "Now the Lord is the Spirit, and where the Spirit of the Lord is, there is freedom."[439]

Of course, there are people who have not struggled as much to submit to the Spirit. They already lived separate from the world; the world did not mean anything to them anymore, and they would have gladly left this life. This was the case with Meister Eckhart,[440] but also with some people in modern times. I already explained that I was in a similar situation.[441] On the other hand, there are people who find it difficult to let go of the world, and they mortify their own flesh to aid themselves in this separation—such as Heinrich Suso.[442]

Finally, it should be mentioned that Patti Gallagher Mansfield had a strong relationship with Mary, the Mother of the Lord. Mary's declaration "I am his servant" in response to the announcement of the angel was the model for giving her life to Christ,[443] and the Magnificat of Mary[444] was her joy in the Spirit. It was this song that she sung during her Baptism in the Holy Spirit.[445] Mary is the "bride of the Spirit";[446] Christ is born in us through the Spirit from the "point" of our soul, as the medieval mystics taught.[447] Also, Mary was there at Pentecost. The Renewal in the Catholic Church has a Marian dimension. Mary is the model.[448]

In connection with her Baptism in the Holy Spirit, Patti Gallagher Mansfield also talks about a renewal of her baptism and Confirmation. She learned that it was through baptism and Confirmation that one received the Holy Spirit. Hence it was important to her to renew her confession of faith—as is customary during the Easter service in the Catholic Church—and open herself to the grace of the sacrament of Confirmation in a new and more comprehensive way. Among Protestants, in contrast, this is not a common practice, and, as mentioned, du Plessis emphasized that the Baptism in the Holy Spirit is administered directly by Jesus Christ.[449] This is why I am of the opinion that the essential ingredient is giving one's life to Christ. Of course, the renewal of baptism and Confirmation cannot hurt, particularly if it is done in connection with giving one's life to Christ.[450]

It remains a fact, however, that in the Catholic Church, the Charismatic Renewal is often connected to the sacraments.

Chapter 10

The Twentieth Century

I do not dare say too much about the end times, not least because the predictions in the Bible are quite complex and not always easily applicable to the trajectory of history as currently known. Still, there are a few thoughts I would like to share.

A. The Time of the Trinity

As discussed earlier, one can say that the history of Israel was the time of God the Father, even though the Holy Spirit was also often active and there were hints of the coming Son. The short time of Jesus Christ's human life was obviously the time of the Son. And since Pentecost, we have been living in the time of the Holy Spirit. Now, however, it seems that all three epochs are coming together. The Jews and other Israelites have gathered again around Jerusalem. There are signs of the second coming of Jesus Christ. More and more often, he appears to this or that Muslim or Jew, leading them to the faith. And, of course, the Holy Spirit is at work as well.

B. The Tribulation

The closer we get to the end, the more active Satan becomes because he knows what will happen to him. We have to expect movements that lead away from Christianity or at least hinder Christianization. This is in part what is happening in the Islamic world, but in Western countries, too, which used to have a Christian emphasis, there are movements that are irreconcilable with Christianity. According to the teachings of David Hathaway, the Tower of Babel has been transferred to Europe, and not only in a physical way but also in its spiritual meaning of people rebelling against God: "The actual physical remnants of the original Babylon, the Ischtar Gate, the 'Gateway to Hell' through which the Jews entered into Babylon as captives, were brought to Germany in 1913 by Kaiser Wilhelm II and erected in Berlin's Pergamon Museum, to join the actual 'Seat of Satan'—Revelation 2:13! This was a temple in Pergamon, Asia Minor, the center of Emperor worship and human sacrifice, the only place in the Bible named as 'Satan's Seat'—also brought to Berlin by Kaiser Wilhelm. In 1902 to celebrate its completion, he ordered a great festival to the pagan gods. In 1934 Hitler had a giant replica of this Seat erected in Nuremberg, and from this place announced the annihilation of the Jews! So the demonic power of the old Babylon and this 'Seat' that we find in the New Testament are transferred to Berlin, and come into our 20th and 21st century, into this generation! In confirmation of this, the death warrant of the Jews was effectively sealed at the 'Seat of Satan', in Germany. Significantly, following the erection of this 'Seat of Satan' in Berlin, there was a great spiritual revival that touched the whole world, an outpouring of the Holy Spirit starting with the Welsh Revival in 1904, then in 1907 and 1908, in Monk Weirmouth in Britain and in Azusa Street in Los Angeles with the manifestation of speaking in tongues! My father was part of this.—But in 1909 the German evangelical churches met in Berlin to discuss this issue—and this is where the devil gets in—they declared that everything to do with the Holy Spirit in this outpouring was of the devil. Evangelical, charismatic German Christians, friends of mine, have 'repented' of this, but the significance is that from that moment, a demonic spirit had entered into Germany. I believe it was this Babylonian spirit that led Germany into two world wars, and into the Holocaust of the Jews. No, it was not the Germans themselves. This same Babylonian spirit has now invaded the European Union. You can clearly see the historic, spiritual link. In 2000 I was absolutely shocked to find that the new European Parliament Building in Strasbourg had been designed by the architects as a replica and copy of the Tower of Babel (Babylon) that you can see in Brueghel's famous depiction of the original tower that was in Iraq. When I asked, they told me that they did this because they intend to finish in Europe, what was started in Babylon! What did they start in Babylon? Rebellion against God! A spirit of rebellion so serious that, to stop them, God confused their tongues and scattered them across the face of the earth! Today there is a 'one world government conspiracy'—to bring nations together again, against God. It's not the men that are directly involved in it, they are controlled by the spirit of Babylon—just as you and I should be controlled by the Holy Spirit."[451]

In this connection, Hathaway does not speak of communism in Russia and its surrounding states. But these, too, revolved around unity and atheism. The goal was not only a political unity but, even more so, an economical unity. There were no longer many companies that could compete with each other freely but only a single economic force, dictated by the state.

To put a disclaimer on Hathaway's portrayal, one should add that the beginning of the European unification actually had Christian roots, initiated by people like Konrad Adenauer in Germany and Robert Schumann in France who signed the Treaty of Rome on March 25, 1957. The goal of the treaty was to finally create peace, particularly between Germany and France.[452] Hathaway overlooks the positive spiritual attitude of these beginnings. But it is true that since then the spiritual direction has changed.[453]

C. Satan Shooting Himself in the Foot

But, as always, when Satan attacks he shoots himself in the foot. That was very clearly the case with the crucifixion of Christ—and in vain did he try to use the wife of Pilate to prevent her husband from issuing the sentence.[454] In a similar way, persecutions of Christians will increase, yet the martyrs will make the crucifixion of Christ real to people, bringing many to the faith. This is already happening. Never before have so many Christians been persecuted. But Satan will see that he has once again only harmed himself, and he will try to reverse his move, as he did with the wife of Pilate.

D. The Secret of Fátima[455]

Pentecostals generally have nothing to do with Marian apparitions and tend to consider them as one of the unacceptable parts of Catholicism. However, the apparitions in 1917 around Fátima, a small village in northern Portugal, are of such significance that they cannot be ignored. The effects they had were clearly from God and cannot be relegated to another spirit.

There, by Fátima, three children experienced a Marian apparition on the thirteenth of every month, starting in May 1917 and ending in October of the same year. The children were Francisco (1908-19) and Jacinta (1910-20) di Marto and their cousin Lucia (1907–2004) Rosa dos Santos. In 1915 and 1916, an angel had already appeared to them on three occasions.[456] The angel revealed himself to be the “angel of peace” and called them to pray, “My God, I believe, I adore, I hope and I love you. I ask pardon of you for those who do not believe, do not adore, do not hope and do not love you.” The angel told them, “Pray thus. The Hearts of Jesus and Mary are attentive to the voice of your supplications.” The angel appeared two more times to them, calling them to prayer and sacrifice.

It was the First World War, which had broken out in 1914. Germans were fighting against Russians while, in March 1917, the communist revolution began in Russia. On April 16, Lenin returned in a closed train wagon from Switzerland via Germany to Russia. On November 6/7, 1917, the putsch of St. Petersburg took place, followed by an armistice with Germany. On October 28, 1918, a mutiny on the High Seas Fleet started a democratic revolution. Emperor William II had to abdicate, and on November 11, 1918, the armistice with the Western powers was signed.

On May 13, 1917, the children experienced their first Marian apparition. Mary told the children that she would return every month on the thirteenth—six more times, and then a seventh time. They were supposed to endure suffering and pray the rosary so that the war would stop. Which is what actually happened.

The third apparition, on July 13, 1917, was the most crucial. Mary started by showing the children a picture of hell, which they described as “a sea of fire; and plunged in this fire were the demons and the souls, as if they were red-hot coals, transparent and black or bronze-colored, with human forms, which floated about in the conflagration, borne by the flames which issued from it with clouds of smoke, falling on all sides as sparks fall in great flagrations—without weight or equilibrium, among shrieks and groans of sorrow and despair which horrified and caused us to shudder with fear."[457] Before this vision, Mary had told them, "Make sacrifices for sinners, and say often, especially while making a sacrifice: O Jesus, this is for love of Thee, for the conversion of sinners, and in reparation for offences committed against the Immaculate Heart of Mary."

And then Mary revealed the second part of the secret to them: "You have seen hell, where the souls of poor sinners go. It is to save them that God wants to establish in the world devotion to my Immaculate Heart. If you do what I tell you, many souls will be saved, and there will be peace. This war will end, but if men do not refrain from offending God, another and more terrible war will begin during the pontificate of Pius XI. When you see a night that is lit by a strange and unknown light, you will know it is the sign God gives you that he is about to punish the world with war and with hunger, and by the persecution of the Church and the Holy Father.—To prevent this, I shall come to the world to ask that Russia be consecrated to my Immaculate Heart, and I shall ask that on the First Saturday of every month Communions of reparation be made in atonement for the sins of the world. If my wishes are fulfilled, Russia will be converted and there will be peace; if not, then Russia will spread her errors throughout the world, bringing new wars and persecution of the Church; the good will be martyred and the Holy Father will have much to suffer; certain nations will be annihilated. But in the end my Immaculate Heart will triumph. The Holy Father will consecrate Russia to me, and she will be converted, and the world will enjoy a period of peace. In Portugal the faith will always be preserved ..."[458]

After that, Mary revealed a third secret to Lucia and Jacinta, which they were not supposed to tell anyone but Francisco.

Also, when they prayed the rosary, they were supposed to say after each "mystery" (ten times the same text), "O my Jesus, forgive us, save us from the fire of hell. Lead all souls to heaven, especially those who are most in need." This is an essential deepening of the usual prayer added to the rosary: "Holy, Mary, Mother of God, pray for us sinners, now and at the hour of our death."

On October 13, 1917, there was a miracle of the sun that was witnessed by many people.[459] As a result, whole processions of repentant people started to walk to Fátima, praying the rosary, especially on the thirteenth of every month.

What should not go unmentioned is that, already on October 23, the Freemasons' lodge of Santarem initiated counter actions against these developments.[460]

The First World War came to an end, but the communist Revolution took over Russia. The Orthodox Church in Russia was pushed against the wall.[461] As early as 1922, twenty-eight bishops and a hundred priests were shot. After the death of Lenin in 1924, Stalin came to power and became sole ruler in 1929. The "League of Militant Atheists" was founded.

On June 13, 1929, Lucia experienced another apparition.[462] It was about eleven o'clock at night, and she saw a light and a picture of the Trinity. Blood of the crucified Son was flowing over a host into a chalice. Under the right arm of the cross stood Mary, under the left were the words "Grace and Mercy." And Lucia heard Mary say, "The moment has come in which God asks the Holy Father to make, in union with all the bishops of the world, the consecration of Russia to my Immaculate Heart, promising to save it by this means ..." Lucia asked others to convey this request to Pope Pius XI, who, in response, celebrated a mass on March 19, 1930, "a mass of atonement, reconciliation and reparation for the many criminal offenses against the Sacred Heart of Jesus and for the liberation of the Russian people, so that the long affliction would finally come to an end," expressly committing the Russian people under the protection of the Mother of God and the saints. This, however, was not enough. The pope also had to conduct a solemn public act, Lucia said, consecrating Russia to the Hearts of Jesus and Mary and calling the bishops of the whole world to do the same. Lucia asked the Lord why Russia could not be converted without such a public consecration. She received the answer, "Because I want my whole Church to recognize that this consecration is a triumph of the Immaculate Heart of Mary, so that it may extend later on, and put the devotion to this Immaculate Heart beside the devotion to my Sacred Heart."

On January 25, 1938, the sky over Europe and North Africa changed its color.[463] Lucia received the information from Mary that this was an announcement of God's judgment because Russia had not been consecrated to her Immaculate Heart. At the same time, Hitler decided to invade Austria, which happened on March 12, 1938. Then, on May 28, 1939, he attacked Czechoslovakia. In August, Germany and Russia signed a non-aggression pact, and Hitler gave the command to attack Poland. Thereupon arose a British-Polish mutual aid pact, and France blocked the Western border. After Germany attacked Poland on September 1, 1939, France and England declared war on Germany on September 3.

On February 10, 1939, Pope Pius XI died. Hesemann calls him a waverer, saying he published his encyclical *With Burning Anxiety* much too late. His successor was Pope Pius XII, who was very devoted to Mary. He had been ordained as bishop on the day of the first apparition in Fátima, on May 13, 1917.

On October 24, 1940,[464] Lucia tried to write the new pope, asking him to conduct the consecration. After the letter had been detained by her bishop, she wrote anew on December 2, 1940. At first, nothing happened. In February 1942, the twenty-fifth anniversary of the apparition in Fátima was celebrated. But it took until October 31, 1942, for Pope Pius XII to make a public address, consecrating the world to the Heart of Mary. On December 8, 1942, he repeated the consecration together with forty cardinals and many bishops, and recommended all bishops and believers to do the same. But the consecration of Russia was only mentioned indirectly.

Still, it was toward the end of 1942 that the war took a decisive turn, the Germans being beaten at the Second Battle of El Alamein in November 1942. On November 8, British and American troops landed in North Africa. On January 31 or February 2, 1943, the German army under General Paulus capitulated in Stalingrad. On May 13, 1943, the Tunesia Campaign came to an end. On May 13, 1944, the victory of Garigliano took place, and Rome was liberated. It is a fact that important events in the war happened on Marian days.[465]

In 1946, the statue of Our Lady of Fátima was sent to travel around the world, starting in Portugal.[466] This was when the "dove miracle" happened. Doves alighted on the statue and remained sitting there for an extended period of time. In France, Freemasons and Republicans protested against the procession of the statue, following which Mary appeared for seven days to children in a suburb of Touraine, asking them to pray for France. Even French bishops did not allow the procession to enter their territory, and the press did not report on the pilgrimage at all. The German bishops joined this policy, so that the procession did not at all take place in Germany.

On May 18, 1948,[467] Lucia joined the Carmelite Order in Coimbra in northern Portugal, thus disappearing as far as the world was concerned. In the Vatican, meanwhile, there were more and more objections to consecrating Russia to the Heart of Mary. The Vatican wanted to start diplomatic relationships with Moscow, hoping to improve the position of Christians under communism. It was feared that a public consecration would hinder such efforts.

From 1949 to 1952, there were Marian apparitions in Heroldsbach (Lower Franconia in Bavaria, Germany), which met with fierce opposition of the bishop there. Though the pope was outraged about the bishop, he did not assert himself against those around him. Then there was a miracle of the sun in the garden of the Vatican when Pius XII proclaimed the bodily ascension of Mary into heaven while her statue of Fátima stood in the garden in front of him (November 1, 1950).

In May of 1952, Lucia experienced another Marian apparition, which caused her to write to the pope once more: "Russia cannot be converted without being consecrated, nor can the world find peace." In response, the pope wrote a "pastoral letter to the people of Russia" on July 7, 1952, in which he mentioned a consecration of the people of Russia. But Lucia was not satisfied. Still, at least Stalin died on March 5, 1953, and his successor Khrushchev turned against Stalinism.

During the pontificates of John XXIII and Paul VI, not much was heard about Fátima. Though both read the third secret that Lucia wrote down in 1944 after another apparition and handed over in a sealed envelope to a bishop in Portugal, who opened it, but closed it again and did not pass it on. The Bishop of Lucia refused to open it himself and finally reached an agreement with Lucia to open it at her death, but no later than 1960. She, herself, made contradictory statements about this at different times. On February 3, 1946: It could not be made known before 1960. On August 12, 1946: The bishop could open it; he would not have to wait until 1960. On October 17, 1946, in answer to the question, "When will the secret be revealed?": "In 1960."—"Why is it necessary to wait that long?"—"Because this is what the Blessed Virgin desires." On May 17, 1955, she made the comment to Cardinal Ottaviani, "The message should not be opened before 1960 … because it will appear much clearer then."[468]

In the beginning of 1957, then, the Congregation for the Doctrine of the Faith requested copies of all the writings of Sister Lucia, particularly of the third secret.

Early in 1959, John XXIII looked into the secret but declared that it did not relate to his own period of office.[469] Pope Paul VI probably read the secret in 1963 and responded the same way as his predecessor.[470] Pope John Paul II only read the secret in the summer of 1981,[471] and for a special reason.

On May 13, 1981, on the anniversary of the first Marian apparition in Fátima sixty-four years earlier, he was wounded by a Turk named Ali Agca who shot at the pope during his weekly appearance on St. Peter's square. The motive was probably related to his activity concerning Poland being subjected to communism.[472] The pope was convinced that Mary had saved him from death.[473] As a result, he asked to be given all documents relating to Fátima, including the third secret, which he received in a sealed envelope on July 18, 1981. He also decided to make a pilgrimage to Fátima on May 13, 1982, and to meet with Sister Lucia. There, during mass, he personally consecrated Russia to the Immaculate Heart of Mary. However, Lucia told him that she thought he had not yet carried out the consecration of Russia in a valid manner. As a result, on December 8, 1983, during the Feast of the Immaculate Conception, the pope sent letters to all the bishops in the world, including those of the Orthodox Church, inviting them to join him in carrying out the consecration of the world to the Immaculate Heart of Mary on the feast of the Annunciation, March 22, 1984.[474] It included the following pronouncement: “Embrace with the love of the Mother and Handmaid of the Lord, this human world of ours, which we entrust and consecrate to you, for we are full of concern for the earthly and eternal destiny of individuals and peoples. In a special way we entrust and consecrate to you those individuals and nations which particularly need to be thus entrusted and consecrated.” Up to this point, it was the text that had been sent. Then, however, he added quietly, “Particularly Russia,” before continuing in a louder voice, “Enlighten especially the peoples whose consecration and entrustment by us you are awaiting.”

Lucia was satisfied.

The subsequent development in Russia took everyone by surprise. On March 11, 1985, Michail Gorbachev became Secretary-General of the Communist Party, and in December 1985 the first meeting with U.S. President Reagan took place regarding the disarmament of nuclear and conventional weapons. In 1987, a process of democratization began, which included the sanctions against religion being lifted.[475]

First in Poland, then in Russia, an anti-communist wave started sweeping the Eastern bloc. On November 9, 1989, the border to the West was opened. On December 1, 1989, Gorbachev went to Rome, to meet with the pope. On October 13, 1990, the anniversary of the Miracle of the Sun, the first religious ceremony took place in the Cathedral of the Dormition in the Kremlin in Moscow since the October Revolution, and on October 14, 1990, the first Orthodox mass in St. Basil’s Basilica in the Red Square since 1917.[476]

On August 19, 1991, communist hardliners revolted in Moscow against President Gorbachev, who was held up in his weekend house in Crimea. Boris Yeltsin, President of the Russian Republic, resisted the rebels and took refuge in the parliament building. Gorbachev stepped down as secretary of the party and President of the Soviet Union. The red flag on top of the Kremlin was replaced with the old blue-white flag of Russia. Taking effect on January 1, 1992, the Soviet Union was changed into the “Commonwealth of Independent States.”[477]

I still remember how there were fears during those events that communism might have a comeback. In the Charismatic Renewal of the Catholic Church in Zurich, we prayed for the situation. Shortly before the prayer, however, I saw a picture before my inner eye: I saw the entire territory of Russia like a giant map, all the way to Vladivostok, and flying over it was an enormous angel with his hands spread out, obviously bringing peace to the region. Much later, I read somewhere that the general in Moscow at the time sent out his troops—fully armed, but without munition. This reminded me of the angel.[478]

E. Answers to Prayer Independent of Fátima

David Hathaway reports how, after the start of the Second World War, the king of England called the British nation seven times to prayer—and that the whole nation prayed.[479] In May of 1940, then, there was first of all the Miracle of Dünkirchen: France and Belgium had capitulated, and the German army had surrounded the English troops in Pas-de-Calais. It is reported that after the British people prayed, a great calm came over the English Channel, which allowed the English troops to cross it on small boats. 330,000 soldiers were saved; only 5,000 died. Then, in the summer of 1940, the German attacked England from the air, destroying its fighter planes on the ground at their military airbase. But once again the British people prayed, and Hitler did not continue his attack, sending his air force elsewhere. Two years later, in 1942, at the Battle of Alamein in North Africa, England had two generals who were true believers, and once again the nation prayed. The British won. Up to that point, they had not won a single battle in this war, but from thereon, they did not lose a single one.

Also, one should not overlook that the Battle of El Alamein started on October 31, 1942, which was the same day that Pope Pius XII consecrated the world to the Heart of Mary.[480]

Finally, we should mention the prayers that took place under the leadership of the Lutheran Pastor Christoph Führer in the Church of St. Nicholas in Leipzig, starting in 1981 and spreading throughout East Germany, even sweeping over to West Germany. Their object was "justice, peace and the conservation of creation." All those who took part in these prayers saw the peaceful opening of the borders of East Germany to West Germany in 1989 as an outflow of their prayers.[481]

Chapter 11

The Future

A. The Catholic Church

We now need to turn to the future of the Catholic Church. I have already made reference to what Christ said about the future of Peter, that is, the pope: "When you grow old, you will stretch out your hands, and someone else will dress you and lead you where you do not want to go."[482] Two days before Pope Benedict XVI announced his resignation, Stefan Driess passed on the following prophecy to a hundred participants in a Charismatic meeting in Rome: "We live at a time in which a strong movement has arisen for the Catholic Church. It will start with a bishop or cardinal making news regarding a special office. … He will be taken from his office or will resign for reasons that are not easily understandable. And this will be a sign that God has started to reposition men and women in the Catholic Church. That which God has already started to prepare in secret with men and women whose hearts beat for the move of the Holy Spirit and the Kingdom of God in the Catholic Church will become visible. We will see movements, including within certain Catholic groups, that will even make some Charismatics envious. Some will even say, 'Why among those people, Lord? Why not among us?' And God will show anew that our Father in heaven does not have such church boundaries; he sees people's hearts, and he is looking for those who seek him earnestly. And those who are humble will even go to learn from people whom they had originally wanted to teach. Those are the people whom God will use. But what they will see isn't something that you can write down conceptually. Rather, it's something that is transferred and kindled spiritually. It won't be dramatic or spectacular, but it will be deep. The things that will be poured out will be deep. It will be different than some of the more spectacular things that have gotten a lot of attention, only to fizzle out again. It will be something deep that will lay a firm foundation in the hearts of the people."[483]

Already back in 1975, Ralph Martin gave a prophecy at the international CE Conference in Rome: "Because I love you, I want to show you what I am doing in the world today. I want to prepare you for what is to come. Days of darkness are coming on the world, days of tribulation. … Buildings that are now standing will not be standing. Supports that are there for my people now will not be there. I want you to be prepared, my people, to know only me and to cleave to me and to have me in a way deeper than ever before. I will lead you into the desert … I will strip you of everything that you are depending on now, so you depend just on me. A time of darkness is coming on the world, but a time of glory is coming for my church, a time of glory is coming for my people. I will pour out on you all the gifts of my Spirit. I will prepare you for spiritual combat; I will prepare you for a time of evangelism that the world has never seen."[484]

It seems to me that the time of the woman in the wilderness is coming to an end, and the Catholic Church will turn into a purely Pentecostal movement. This is also in line with what David Hathaway said at an Israel conference in London on February 23, 2013:[485] "We live in very troubled times. According to some prophecies this new Pope will be the last![486] It is possible that Rome could unite with other faiths and create a single 'world church' with its headquarters in Jerusalem. Could that mean the rebuilding of the Temple? And who will be the Antichrist? God only knows."

In this connection, what is known as the "Ecclesia Revival" should also be mentioned: "Since the year 2000, many new Christian communities have formed all over Europe. Often, these groups were started by 'ordinary' Christians, without interference by church leaders. This is also true of the Catholic Church. The Dutch journalist Theo van de Kerkhof explored seven of these new communities. A hundred to four hundred people come to their weekly services, which they call simply 'celebrations.' They do feel connected to the Catholic Church but also enjoy their freedom. They are rooted in the Bible, are involved in social initiatives, and their spirituality is welcoming to everyone. The bishops try to downplay the significance of these groups, but Franck Ploum, leader of an ecumenical center in Amsterdam, speaks of a true 'Ecclesia Revival.'"

B. The Third Secret of Fátima[488]

On May 13, 2000, Pope John Paul II visited Fátima a second time. At the end of a mass that lasted two and a half hours, during which Sister Lucia received Holy Communion from the hand of the pope, he had Cardinal Sodano announce the third secret, in Portuguese. On June 26, 2000, it was officially published in Rome through Cardinal Joseph Ratzinger and Archbishop Tarcisio Bertone of the Congregation for the Doctrine of the Faith. The English translation of Sister Lucia's transcription is as follows.

"After the two parts which I have already explained, at the left of Our Lady and a little above, we saw an Angel with a flaming sword in his left hand; flashing, it gave out flames that looked as though they would set the world on fire; but they died out in contact with the splendor that Our Lady radiated towards him from her right hand: pointing to the earth with his right hand, the Angel cried out in a loud voice, 'Penance, Penance, Penance!'

And we saw in an immense light that is God: 'something similar to how people appear in a mirror when they pass in front of it' a Bishop dressed in White. 'We had the impression that it was the Holy Father.' Other Bishops, Priests, men and women of religious orders going up a steep mountain, at the top of which there was a big Cross of rough-hewn trunks as of a cork-tree with the bark; before reaching there the Holy Father passed through a big city half in ruins and half trembling with halting step, afflicted with pain and sorrow, he prayed for the souls of the corpses he met on his way; having reached the top of the mountain, on his knees at the foot of the big Cross he was killed by a group of soldiers who fired bullets and arrows at him, and in the same way there died one after another the other Bishops, Priests, men and women of religious orders, and various laypeople of different ranks and positions. Beneath the two arms of the Cross there were two Angels each with a crystal aspersorium in his hand, in which they gathered up the blood of the

Martyrs and with it sprinkled the souls that were making their way to God."

There are many different interpretations, particularly after the attack of September 11, 2001, in New York. However, I would like to suggest an interpretation that, to my knowledge, has not yet been advanced by anyone: It is a symbolic depiction of the replacement of the Catholic Church by the Pentecostal movement. It is about the end of the woman's time in the wilderness, in line with Revelation 12. The following arguments support this view:

The year 1960 plays a role in the publication. That is about the same time as the Second Vatican Council and the start of the Charismatic Renewal in the Catholic Church.

Bishops and priests are "killed." This is the end of the ordination of priests and the beginning of an even stronger blowing of the Holy Spirit.

Laypersons, too, are killed. That is the end of people in the church basing their faith entirely on the actions of ordained priests.

The dead leave their blood. As always, the blood of the martyrs makes the cross of Christ real to people, generally leading to new believers.

In the center is the hill with the cross, surrounded by the city of Rome: As the successor of Peter, the Bishop of Rome is the rock, which will continue to exist in a different form, his hands stretched out, and he is being girded by someone else. This means the bishop dressed in white will no longer be called pope.

Pope Francis I is a precursor of this development. He is friend with Pentecostals. He has taken the name of Francis, the saint of the new Spirit.

The development is far removed from those who rejected the Second Vatican Council, particularly Bishop Lefevre. One of his supporters wanted to stab Pope John Paul II to death when he was in Fátima.[489]

I am not saying, though, that this has to be the only interpretation of the third secret. It is entirely possible that there will also be an actual attack on the Vatican—probably not through a conventional military action but by a terrorist organization, as is currently being feared.

C. The Lord Returns after the End of the Catholic Church

I refer to Matthew 24:29: "Immediately after the tribulation of those days, the sun will be darkened, and the moon will not give its light, and the stars will fall from the sky, and the powers of the heavens will be shaken."[490]

One can relate this text to the woman in the wilderness. The sun (the light of the Lord) darkens; the moon (the church) does not give its light; and the twelve stars (the successors of the twelve Apostles, that is, the ordained priests) fall down from her head. One question that is still not clear to me is what is meant by "the powers of the heavens." It cannot mean the Holy Spirit, since he will only get stronger after the Catholic Church has disappeared, and particularly when the Lord returns. Starting in verse 30, we then read, "And then the sign of the Son of Man will appear in heaven, and all the tribes of the earth will mourn, and they will see the Son of Man coming upon the clouds of heaven with power and great glory." The Lord will return with the clouds the way he went. According to this text, it seems that the period in which the Pentecostal movement has entirely replaced the Catholic Church will be very short. Maybe this is what is meant by the shaking of the powers of the heavens.

D. Faith Today

The hardships of the twentieth century—communism, National Socialism, and probably also atheistic freemasonry—have their roots in the nineteenth century or earlier. In the twentieth century, then, there were increasingly questions about the meaning of life, driving people into drug addiction and experiences with death as the solution. Possibly, the life goal of Islamic terrorists also falls under this category. Let me lay out this development in greater detail.

I will start with an account of a pagan mystic (born about A.D. 125) devoted to the goddess Isis:

"There then followed a preparation lasting ten days. I obeyed his [the Chief Priest's] instructions in all reverence and at last the day came for taking my vows. As evening approached a crowd of priests came flocking to me from all directions, each one giving me congratulatory gifts, as the ancient custom is. Then the Chief Priest invested me in a new linen garment and led me by the hand into the inner recesses of the adytum itself. I have no doubt, curious reader, that you are eager to know what happened when I entered. However, not wishing to leave you, if you are religiously inclined, in a state of tortured suspense, I will recall as much as I may. I approached the very gates of death and put one foot on Prosperine's threshold; yet was I permitted to return, rapt through all the elements. At midnight I saw the sun shining as if it were noon; I entered the presence of the deities of the under-world and the deities of the upper-world, stood near and honored them. See, now I have given you a report. You have heard, but you do not necessarily understand. So let me tell you what one may tell the uninitiated without thereby committing a sin.

The solemn rites ended at dawn and I emerged from the adytum wearing twelve different stoles, certainly a most holy costume. ... In my right, I carried a flaming torch, and my head was adorned with a crown of palms whose glimmering leaves stood out like beams of light. Being thus decked as the picture of the sun, I stood still like a statue, until the curtains were pulled aside and I was suddenly exposed to the gaze of the crowd. Then the celebration of my birth as an initiate began [*festissimus natalis sacrorum*]."[491]

What this man experienced at the hands of these priests is a path to death, getting a foretaste of the world beyond. This is mysticism. Mysticism is always connected to asceticism, a renouncement of the world. What this man did provides an answer to the question of the meaning of existence. Meaningful existence always stands in relation to the beyond, making it an eternal existence that receives meaning from the beings in the beyond.

It seems that the question about the meaning of existence actually grows with the general de-Christianization of today. In Germany, it particularly came to the fore after the First World War, being formulated at first by philosophers. Martin Heidegger gave expression to this in his book *Being and Time*, published in 1927, though Heidegger's mode of expressing himself makes it difficult to quote him. I therefore rely on I.M. Bochenski and his book *Contemporary European Philosophy*, which is based on lectures given in the winter semester of 1945/46 to American military students, subsequently published in French. I cite here the second edition, published in 1951, with widely expanded expositions about Jean-Paul Sartre:[492] "The very being of human existence is being-unto-death. … It is this self-same fact which throws human existence into dread, and leads it to flee into the world."[493] The true "I" seeks to escape into the general "one" (German: *Man*). "*Man* does not allow himself to think of his own death but simply says 'one has to die' (*man stirbt*)."[494]

Bochenski primarily discusses Sartre's seminal work, *Being and Nothingness*, which appeared in 1943.[495] Sartre's conclusion is the "non-existence" of man. The ethical consequence of this is the denial of any objective values or laws, the assertion of the absolute meaninglessness of human existence (death, too, is rejected as its meaning) and the disavowal of the seriousness of life.[496] Bochenski does not mention that the only purpose that Sartre saw in life was extreme sensuality in all directions (like Heidegger's "fleeing into the world")[497].

Finally, we should also mention Albert Camus ("The Myth of Sisyphus," including the appendix "Hope and the Absurd in the work of Franz Kafka," 75. edition, Paris 1942). *"L'absurde et le suicide: Il n'y a qu'un problème philosophique vraiment sérieux: c'est le suicide."*[498] *"Juger que la vie vaut ou ne vaut pas la peine d'être vécue, c'est répondre à la question fondamentale de la philosophie."*[499] *"Ce divorce entre l'homme et sa vie, l'acteur et son décor, c'est proprement le sentiment de l'absurdité."*[500]

Obviously, all these philosophers have a sense that, apart from the enjoyments of this world, death opens a dimension that might also bring gain. This attitude also seems to be the foundation of movements such as National Socialism. On the surface, it is a this-worldly, collective sense of fulfillment, but behind it is the possibility of death. Hitler commanded his generals not to negotiate with the enemy in hopeless situations but to keep fighting to the bitter end. He, himself, ended his life by suicide. But even without such collective movements, there are many individuals today who try to experience the border of death. During my legal studies in Zuriech, a criminalist gave a lecture in which he talked about people who have a guillotine whose blade is attached to a rope that stops it just when it touches the throat of the person. When this goes wrong, it is difficult to decide whether one should classify this as suicide, murder, or an accident. Less dangerous is bungee jumping. People jump from high places while being secured with a rope that pulls them back up just before hitting the ground. Consuming drugs basically has the same effect. In his book *Ich steige hinab in die Barke der Sonne: Alt-ägyptische Meditationen zu Tod und Auferstehung in Bezug auf Joh 20-21* ("I Descend into the Boat of the Sun: Ancient Egyptian Meditations on Death and Resurrection in Light of John 20-21"),[501] Eugen Drewermann cites an author who proves this. Drewermann basically tries to harmonize the religion of ancient Egypt with Christianity and depth psychology. Then he quotes from a book by the Indian shaman Carlos Castaneda, *Separate Reality*:[502] "Only the idea of death makes a man sufficiently detached so he is incapable of abandoning himself to anything. Only the idea of death makes a man sufficiently detached so he can't deny himself anything. A man of that sort, however, does not crave, for he has acquired a silent lust for life and for all things of life. He knows his death is stalking him and won't give him time to cling to anything, so he tries, without craving, all of everything."[503] "Death is the whisper of Mescalito in your ears."[504] "Death has two stages. The first is a blackout. It is a meaningless stage, very similar to the first effect of Mescalito, in which one experiences a lightness that makes one feel happy, complete, and that everything in the world is at ease. But that is only a shallow state; it soon vanishes and one enters a new realm, a realm of harshness and power. That second stage is the real encounter with Mescalito. Death is very much like this. The first stage is a shallow blackout. The second, however, is the real stage where one meets with death; it is a brief moment, after the first blackout, when we find that we are, somehow, ourselves again. It is then that death smashes against us with quiet fury and power until it dissolves our lives into nothing."[505] "[Death] would enter inside you with uncontrollable force and would make you expand; it would make you flat and extend you over the sky and the earth and beyond. And you would be like a fog of tiny crystals moving, moving away."[506] Finally, one can put Islamic suicide bombers in this group as well, killing both themselves and non-Islamists. Islamists do not believe that they can predict anything about what Allah will do, as he is so much greater and more significant than they. That is why, in principle, it will always remain uncertain whether they will go to heaven, and the heaven in which they do believe is quite this-worldly. Jesus said, "I am the way and the truth and the life. No one comes to the Father except through me" (John 14:6). Islamists do not believe that Jesus Christ is the Son of God, only acknowledging him as a prophet who was superseded by Muhammad. Nevertheless, most terrorists are convinced that their suicide is a certain route to "heaven."

All these methods of getting close to death lead people to the border of the beyond, into a dimension of their existence that imbues their life with meaning because it is the door to eternal life and a kingdom that is not of this world. At this door, however, it is still uncertain whether it is eternal damnation or eternal bliss that is waiting on the other side. People come close to heavenly spirits—but also evil spirits. Since Jesus Christ has come to earth, it is mostly evil spirits that one meets through such means. Drug abuse illustrates this well. Experts differentiate between a physical addiction and a psychological one. Even when physical addiction has been overcome, the psychological addiction can resurface even after a prolonged period of time. Actually, it is spiritual in nature; the evil spirits return whenever they please.

This shows that access to the beyond should not be achieved through such methods but only through Jesus Christ. He implies this in a parable as conveyed by the Evangelist John (10:7f.): "Amen, amen, I say to you, I am the gate for the sheep. All who came (before me) are thieves and robbers, but the sheep did not listen to them. I am the gate. Whoever enters through me will be saved, and will come in and go out and find pasture. A thief comes only to steal and slaughter and destroy; I came so that they might have life and have it more abundantly."

Indeed, instead of doing bungee jumping, it is much better to completely die with Jesus Christ, who died for us a bloody death so that we can rise with him to gain access to the dimension of the Holy Spirit, finding eternal life in the kingdom of God were evil spirits have no place.

The question of what it means to die and rise with Jesus Christ is the mystery of faith. It is a knowledge of the beyond that only believers know and *can* know. Again, it is the Evangelist John who hints at this process (12:1f.). Six days before Passover—on which Jesus was crucified—Jesus visited Lazarus, whom he had raised from the dead. There, John tells us, "Mary took a liter of costly perfumed oil made from genuine aromatic nard and anointed the feet of Jesus and dried them with her hair; the house was filled with the fragrance of the oil. Then Judas the Iscariot, one (of) his disciples, and the one who would betray him, said, 'Why was this oil not sold for three hundred days' wages and given to the poor?' He said this not because he cared about the poor but because he was a thief and held the money bag and used to steal the contributions. So Jesus said, 'Leave her alone. Let her keep this for the day of my burial. You always have the poor with you, but you do not always have me.'" Mary stands for the female part of Lazarus' soul, able to believe in order to die with Jesus. The nard oil is already mentioned in the Song of Songs; it is something that connects the woman to her lover.[507]

When it comes to the meaning of life, Satan again shoots himself in the foot. Experiencing the meaninglessness of life does not necessarily lead to destructive paths and the direction of the esoteric and occult but can also lead to Jesus Christ. It is no longer Mary who is our protector and helper; now we have a direct relationship with Jesus Christ. This could already be seen in Fátima when Mary said we should pray to Jesus Christ, but Sister Faustina Kowalska (1905--1938) of Glogowiec near Lodz in Poland makes this point even more clearly. I feel prompted to replicate here what I wrote in my book *Das Nardenöl aus dem Alabastergefäss* ("The Nard Oil from the Alabaster Jar") about her. By putting her in connection with the Pentecostal movement, she gains a whole new significance:

E. Sister Faustina Kowalska

The efforts of the Catholic Church regarding the devotion to the Sacred Heart of Jesus are one thing, but the direct intervention of the Lord is another matter. "I myself will pasture my sheep"[508] is also true within the Catholic Church, and it is necessarily all the more true when we consider all believers in Christ, the whole body of Christ, and even those who do not yet believe whom our Father in heaven wants to give to Jesus Christ in future. In line with this, the Lord revealed himself before the Second World War to a Polish nun, giving the devotion to the Sacred Heart of Jesus a new, more contemporary form.

The nun was Sister Mary Faustina Kowalska (1905–1938) of Glogowiec near Lodz,[509] who had a close personal relationship with God and regularly talked to the Lord while he appeared to her in visions. Following the instruction of the Lord and the advice of her father confessors, she kept a diary about these conversations.[510] The message she passed on ties in with a picture of the Heart of the Lord. However, it is no longer represented in a stylized way with a crown of thorns, cross, and a flame of fire, but with two rays that emanate from the wound of the Heart: a red ray and a pale, colorless one. The right hand of the Lord is raised in blessing; the left points to the place of the wound of the Heart from which the rays emanate, his gaze following the beams.[511] Below the picture, it says, "Jesus, I trust in you." Faustina received from the Lord a detailed explanation of the picture:[512] "The two rays denote Blood and Water. The pale ray stands for the Water which makes souls righteous. The red ray stands for the Blood which is the life of soul … These two rays issued forth from the very depths of my tender mercy when my agonized Heart was opened by a lance on the Cross. These rays shield souls from the wrath of my Father. Happy is the one who will dwell in their shelter, for the just hand of God shall not lay hold of him. I desire that the first Sunday after Easter be the Feast of Mercy. … Mankind will not have peace until it turns with trust to my mercy. Oh, how much I am hurt by a soul's distrust! Such a soul professes that I am holy and just, but does not believe that I am Mercy and does not trust in my Goodness. Even the devils glorify my Justice but do not believe in my Goodness. My Heart rejoices in this title of Mercy. Proclaim that mercy is the greatest attribute of God.[513] All the works of my hands are crowned with mercy."

This picture is more biblical[514] and also more modern, particularly the original picture that, according to Faustina Kowalska, was later falsified. It is a call to accept redemption, pure and simple. In contrast to the picture of the Sacred Heart of Jesus, it is not the suffering Christ that takes priority but his mercy. The message of the picture strongly opposes the view of seeing Jesus only as a stern judge.[515] Without saying this explicitly, what is rejected is the view common among some Catholics to the effect that one needs the intercession of Mary, the merciful Mother of

Jesus, to appease Jesus. Faustina writes very clearly, "Jesus, I know that your goodness surpasses the goodness of the most tender mother."[516] This is all the more significant because Faustina belonged to the "Congregation of the Sisters of Our Lady of Mercy." But she heard from the Lord himself emphasizing his great mercy:[517] "I desire that priests proclaim this great mercy of mine towards souls of sinners. Let the sinner not be afraid to approach me. The flames of mercy are burning me—clamoring to be spent; I want to pour them out upon these souls."[518]

Rooted in the message of the mercy of God there grows a worship that allows God to change us, which means that it is truly worship of God. Jesus is received as the one who changes our hearts. Thus, Faustina writes, "I begged for his mercy that he might heal and purify my poor soul. Then I heard these words, *'My daughter, all your miseries have been consumed in the flame of my love, like a little twig thrown into a roaring fire. By humbling yourself in this way, you draw upon yourself and upon other souls an entire sea of my mercy.'*[519] I answered, 'Jesus, mold my poor heart according to your divine delight.'" *"And,"* she heard Jesus say, *"your heart is my constant dwelling place, despite the misery that you are. I united myself with you, take away your misery and give you my mercy. I perform works of mercy in every soul. The greater the sinner, the greater the right he has to my mercy."*[520] And Faustina sings: "O most sweet Jesus, who have deigned to allow miserable me to gain a knowledge of your unfathomable mercy; O most sweet Jesus, who have graciously demanded that I tell the whole world of your incomprehensible mercy, this day I take into my hands the two rays that spring from your merciful Heart; that is, the Blood and the Water; and I scatter them all over the globe so that each soul may receive your mercy and, having received it, may glorify it for endless ages. O most sweet Jesus who, in your incomprehensible kindness, have deigned to unite my wretched heart to your most merciful Heart, it is with your own Heart that I glorify God, our Father, as no soul has ever glorified him before." Worthy of consideration are also the following words of Jesus, "One thing alone is necessary: that the sinner set ajar the door of his heart, be it ever so little, to let in a ray of God's merciful grace, and then God will do the rest."[521]

It is true that people need to be willing, but God is the one who enables them, in line with the blessing of Mary. Driven, then, by the Spirit, and not because of any requirements of the convent, Faustina formulated the following prayer in which she dedicated her life to Christ: "Jesus-Host [that is, the bread of Holy Communion], whom I have this very moment received into my heart, through this union with you I offer myself to the heavenly Father as a sacrificial Host, abandoning myself totally and completely to the most merciful and holy will of my God. From today onward, your will, Lord, is my food. Take my whole being; dispose of me as you please. Whatever your fatherly hand gives me, I will accept with submission, peace and joy. I fear nothing, no matter in what direction you lead me; helped by your grace I will carry out everything you demand of me."[522]

*

However, Faustina's experiences of the mercy of the Lord did not only cause her joy but also much suffering. Like a martyr, she made the suffering of Christ real for her generation. Yet Faustina knew that it was always the cross of Christ, not her own suffering, that brought salvation. In fact it is the Heart of Christ in her, which carries the suffering. She heard: "There is but one price at which souls are brought, and that is suffering united to my suffering on the cross."[523] Accordingly, she says, "It is my constant endeavor to plead for mercy for the world. I unite myself closely with Jesus and stand before him as an atoning sacrifice on behalf of the world. God will refuse me nothing when I entreat him with the voice of his son. My sacrifice is nothing in itself ..."[524]

*

Faustina received a short prayer from the Lord that she should repeat over and over again. Though it is called the "rosary of mercy," it is addressed to the Father and has nothing to do with Mary. In typically Catholic style, it starts as follows:

"Eternal Father, I offer you the Body and Blood, Soul and Divinity of your dearly beloved Son, our Lord Jesus Christ for the expiction of our sins and those of the whole world."

What is meant is that by becoming one with the sacrifice of Christ on the cross I receive the grace that flows out of it in a stream that is not just supposed to reach me but, through me, all other sinners. This is my sacrifice. This prayer can be seen as a confirmation of Pope Leo XIII consecrating the whole world to the Sacred Heart of Jesus.

After this beginning of the prayer, which ensures that the rest of the prayer is rooted in the redemptive act of Jesus, what is basically the request Bartimaeus made of Jesus is repeated several times in different words, addressed to God the Father:

"For the sake of his [Jesus'] sorrowful Passion have mercy on us and on the whole world."

Again, Jesus' work of redemption is expressly stated. The gospel has already been preached to the poor who cried for mercy. Also, the request is extended to the whole world. While Faustina was absorbed in this prayer, she heard the following:

"Oh, what great graces I will grant to souls who say this chaplet; the very depths of my tender mercy are stirred for the sake of those who say the chaplet. Write down these words, my daughter. Speak to the world about my mercy; let all mankind recognize my unfathomable mercy. It is a sign for the end times; after it will come the day of justice. While there is still time, let them have recourse to the fount of my mercy; let them profit from the Blood and Water which gushed forth for them."[526]

*

Toward the end of her life, Faustina started to feel more strongly that she should found her own order, but this turned out to be impossible due to her health. As a Catholic, one is tempted to see this as a preparation for her intercessory role in heaven. Hence, she writes, "I feel certain that my mission will not come to an end upon my death, but will begin. O doubting souls, I will draw aside for you the veils of heaven to convince you of God's goodness, so that you will no longer continue to wound with your distrust the sweetest Heart of Jesus. God is Love and Mercy."[527] And when one considers what she heard from the Lord about this new order, it stands to reason that she will pray for Protestants. Toward the end of her life, at least, the Lord gave her promises that seem to point to events within Protestantism.[528] After she died, an order based on her thoughts was actually founded,[529] but that alone cannot really be the fulfillment of what she wrote. Even back in 1935, Faustina received the following directive:

"... such a congregation be founded as soon as possible, and you shall live in it together with your companions. My Spirit shall be the rule of your life. Your life is to be modeled on mine, from the crib to my death on the cross. Penetrate my mysteries, and you will know the abyss of my mercy towards creatures and my unfathomable goodness—and this you shall make known to the world. Through your prayers, you shall mediate between heaven and earth."[530]

These principles do not look like those of a Catholic order but rather of a Protestant community or congregation. What is striking is the basis for this community: the Holy Spirit and the Bible (the Gospels) as well as the proclamation of the mercy of God through the cross.

It is also significant that Faustina feared to lose the protection of Mary because of this vision for a new order.[531] She does not know that she will go with Protestants, but she suspects that she will be without Mary.

Again she received directives about the new order: "In his hands He was holding a white garment with which he clothed me and a cord with which he girded me, and he covered me with a red cloak like the one he was clothed with during his Passion and a veil of the same color, and he said to me, *'This is how you and your companions are going to be clothed. My life from birth to death on the Cross will be the rule for you. Fix your eyes upon me and live according to what you see. I desire that you penetrate into my spirit more deeply and understand that I am meek and humble of heart.'"*[532]

The garment should be understood symbolically, first the christening robe and then, in this power of the Lord, the suffering.

In 1937, Faustina wrote, "Today, I saw how the Holy Mysteries were being celebrated without liturgical vestments and in private homes, because of a passing storm; and I saw the sun come out from the Blessed Sacrament, and all other lights went out, or rather, they were dimmed; and all the people were looking toward this [one] light. But at the present time I do not understand the meaning of this vision."[534] The storm may be the persecution of the church, perhaps at the hands of the Nazis in Poland or, more likely, at the hands of the communists. But it may also be a picture of an evangelical Communion in a house church.

And, finally, she hears:

"Today bring to me the souls of heretics and schismatics, and immerse them in the ocean of my mercy. During my bitter Passion they tore at my Body and Heart; that is, my Church. As they return to unity with the Church, my wounds heal, and in this way they alleviate my Passion."[534]

It can hardly be denied that Faustina is relevant for evangelically-minded Christians and that, through her, God himself renewed and deepened Pope Leo XIII's consecration of the world to the Sacred Heart of Jesus. In his encyclical *Dives in Misericordia* of 1966, Pope John Paul II took up the revelations of Jesus to Faustina Kowolska. In 1993, he beatified her, and on April 30, 2000, she was canonized. At the same time, the Sunday after Easter was declared to be the "Divine Mercy Sunday." Prior to this, the Sunday was known as "White Sunday," not because First Communion usually takes place then and the girls often come dressed in white bridal clothes but because adults used to be baptized on Easter and wore their white christening robes until the next Sunday. Hence, the day of the mercy of God is rightly related to baptism and Communion. So far, however, Catholics at large have taken little note of all of this, perhaps because Faustina Kowalska is the patron saint of Protestants, primarily of the Pentecostal and Evangelical movement, which is experiencing such a massive growth today.

F. Pope Francis I and His Relationship to Pentecostalism

Even as Archbishop Mario Jorge Bergoglio of Buenos Aires, Pope Francis I had friendly relations with the non-Catholic Charismatic Renewal. One example is Tony Palmer from South Africa.[535] When he became a believer in 1992, it is told that, together with his wife, he knocked on about three thousand doors in his part of town, sharing his faith. He completed a theological training and became the African-wide leader of a Christian organization, after which he felt called by God to go to Italy and engage in missionary activities within the Catholic Church. He waited for the Catholic Church to invite him, and in 2003 he actually received an e-mail from the Charismatic Renewal saying that Charismatic Catholics had been aware of his work and were wondering if he might want to come to Italy. In Italy, then, Tony Palmer became an

Anglican priest and bishop of the "Order of the Ark Community," an international, ecumenical, Christ-centered and Charismatic community that has taken up the spirituality of the Celtic church and that of Francis of Assisi. Around the year 2006, Tony Palmer traveled to Argentina with the goal of working among the Catholics there too. His first step was to get in contact with the local bishop, which happened to be Pater Bergoglio. They became friends, even quite close friends. Bergoglio washed the feet of Protestant pastors, and Charismatic pastors prayed for the Catholic bishops to receive the Baptism in the Holy Spirit.

After Christmas of 2013, Tony Palmer received a phone call from Pater Bergoglio, now Pope Francis. He asked his friend Tony to visit him on his next stop in Italy. During this occasion, they recorded a video.[536] Clearly, the pope is for ecumenism and charismata.[537]

On July 28, 2014, Pope Francis visited the Pentecostal pastor Giovanni Traettino in Caserta, Naples, and his church.[538] About 350 believers were gathered there, among them 150 guests from Italy, the United States, Canada, Argentina, Spain, France, and India who had all followed Traettino's invitation to come to Caserta. Pope Francis told the people gathered there, "Catholics were among those who persecuted and denounced the Pentecostals as overly emotional 'enthusiasts,' almost as if they were crazy people who corrupted the human race. I am the shepherd of the Catholics and I ask you to forgive my Catholic brothers and sisters who did not understand and were tempted by the devil, doing the same thing that Joseph's brothers did. I ask the Lord to give us the grace to come to see this, and to forgive … Thank you!" In response, Traettino said that the pope had given the Pentecostal movement a great and unexpected gift—a gift that almost seemed unthinkable before.

However, it should be noted that the Caholic Church has officially never decried Pentecostalism as a "sect", although some bishops did not share this attidude, particularly in South America. Since 1972, there have been regular dialogues and discussions between the Pontifical Council for the Union of Christians and leading representatives of Pentecostal churches and important personalities in the Charismatic movement within Evangelical and Anglican churches. I refer the reader to the edition of Norbert Baumert and Gerhard Bially regarding *Pflingstler und*

Katholiken im Dialog: Die vier Abschlussberichte einer internationalen Kommission aus 25 Jahren ("Dialogue between Pentecostals and Catholics: Four Final Reports from 25 Years of an International Commission.")[540] It is noteworthy that in the last chapter (VI: Common Testimony) of the last report (par. 123f., p. 91f.) there is a call to mutual forgiveness, which is exactly what the pope has now done.

In the end, I would like to again refer to the work of Arnold Bittlinger who gives a detailed account (484 pages) of the discussion about the first session in Horgen at Lake Zuriech, ten miles outside of Zuriech.[541]

Notes

[1] Barrett, David B. & Kurian, George T. & Johnson, Todd M. *World Christian Encyclopedia*, 2nd Edition. Oxford: 2001 (Barrett, *Encyclopedia*).

[2] Burgess, Stanley M. & Van der Maas, Eduard M. *The New International Dictionary of Pentecostal and Charismatic Movements*, 2nd Edition. Grand Rapids, Michigan: 2003 (Burgess, *Dictionary*).

[3] Barrett, Encyclopedia, Vol. I, p. 4

[4] Burgess, Dictionary, p. 289 par.67–75

[5] Burgess, Dictionary, p. 58

[6] Burgess, Dictionary, pp. 63f.; cf. p. 297 par. 35

[7] Cf. Barrett, Encyclopedia, Vol. I, p. 11

[8] Joel 2:23

[9] Joel 3:1f.

[10] Jam 5:7. Translation based on Greek Interlinear Bible: http://www.scripture4all.org/OnlineInterlinear/Greek_Index.htm.

[11] Bartleman, Frank. *Azusa Street: How Pentecost Came to Los Angeles*. Bridge-Logos 1980 – EasyRead Large 16 (Bartleman, Azusa Street) p. i and p. xvii.

[12] Ephraim, Bruder. *Nachsommerregen. Der Löwe von Juda: Die Geburt einer neuen Gemeinschaft*. Münsterschwarzbach: 1987 (Ephraim, *Nachsommerregen*).

[13] Prigent, Pierre. *Apocalypse 12, Histoire de l'exégèse*, in: *Beiträge zur Geschichte biblischer Exegese, Bd. 2*. Tübingen: 1959 (Prigent, *Apocalypse 12*).

[14] Prigent, Apocalypse 12, pp. 3f.

[15] "Parée d'un éclat céleste"

[16] Prigent, Apocalypse 12, pp. 10f.

[17] Prigent, Apocalypse 12, p. 15

[18] Prigent, Apocalypse 12, pp. 23f.

[19] Prigent, Apocalypse 12, pp. 24 & 26

[20] Prigent, Apocalypse 12, p. 26

[21] Prigent, Apocalypse 12, pp. 77f.

[22] Kamlah, Dr. Wilhelm. *Apokalypse und Geschichtstheologie. Die mittelalterliche Auslegung der Apokalypse vor Joachim von Fiore*. Berlin: 1935 (Kamlah, *Apokalypse*), pp. 130f.

[23] I leave out the supporting quotes, since they are difficult to find, given the available information.

[24] Rahner, Hugo: *Symbole der Kirche: Die Ekklesiologie der Väter*. Salzburg: 1964, p. 13.

[25] 2Tim 1:6

[26] 2Tim 1:13f.

[27] Cf. Acts 14:22f.; 6:6; 1Tim 4:14 & 5:22.

[28] Cf. Ott, Ludwig: *Grundriss der Dogmatik,* 11. Ed., Bonn 2010 (Ott, *Dogmatik*), pp. 254f.; 385f.; 440f.; 621f. (Ott, Ludwig: *Fundamentals of Catholic Dogma*. TAN Books, 1992)

[29] Cf. "Apostolizität der Kirche" in Kuhn, Wolfgang: *Lexikon für Theologie und Kirche*, 2nd Edition, Freiburg i. Br.: 1964 (LThK).

[30] Cf. e.g. Joh 3:6: "What is born of spirit is spirit."

[31] Franzen, August. *Kleine Kirchengeschichte* (Herderbücherei 237), 7th Edition. Freiburg i. Br.: 1978 (Franzen, *Kirchengeschichte*), p. 4.

[32] Mk 16:16

[33] Ott, Dogmatik, p. 492f.

[34] Ott, Dogmatik, p. 490f.

[35] Ott, Dogmatik, p. 490f.

[36] Franzen, Kirchengeschichte, pp. 46f.

[37] Franzen, Kirchengeschichte, p. 47–49.

[38] 1Tim 1:4; 4:7; 6:4; 6:20; Col 2:8f.; Acts 2:6; 2:15

[39] Ch. XI, D. Faith Today

[40] Franzen, Kirchengeschichte, p. 49

[41] Franzen, Kirchengeschichte, pp. 49f.

[42] Franzen, Kirchengeschichte, p. 50

[43] Franzen, Kirchengeschichte, pp. 50f.

[44] Franzen, Kirchengeschichte, pp. 51f.

[45] Mk 16:16

[46] Ott, Dogmatik, pp. 492f.

[47] Acts 16:15; 16:33

[48] Ott, Dogmatik, pp. 490f.

[49] Joel 3:1f.

[50] Rev 14:1–5

[51] Friedell, Egon: *Kulturgeschichte Ägyptens und des Alten Orients*, 3.Aufl. München 1980 (*Kulturgeschichte Ägyptens*), p. 140.

[52] Posener, Georges. *Lexikon der ägyptischen Kultur*, Wiesbaden 1960(?) (Posener, *ägyptische Kultur*). pp. 180f.

[53] Ex 3:21f.; 11:2f.; 12:35f.; Ps 105:37

[54] Cf. Wendelborn, Franz. *Gott und Geschichte: Joachim von Fiore und die Hoffnung der Christenheit*. Leipzig: 1974 (Wendelborn, *Joachim von Fiore*), pp. 7f.

[55] Mt 1:1f.

[56] Latin text: Grundmann, Herbert. *Studien über Joachim von Floris* (Beiträge zur Kulturgeschichte des Mittelalters und der Renaissance, herausgegeben von Walter Goetz, Band 32). Leipzig/Berlin: 1927 (Grundmann, *Studien*), pp. 20f.

[57] Mk 13:32; Mt 24:36; Acts 1:7; Ott, Dogmatik, pp. 658f.

[58] Joel 2:23; James 5:7; Interlinear Bible

[59] Wendelborn, Joachim von Fiore, pp. 29f.; Grundmann, Studien, pp. 129f.

[60] Wendelborn, Joachim von Fiore, p. 29

[61] Ex 33:11; Deut 34:10; 5:4; Gen 32:31 (Jacob)

[62] Wendelborn, Joachim von Fiore, pp. 29f.

[63] Wendelborn, Joachim von Fiore, p. 39

[64] Mt 12:31f.; Mk 3:28f; Lk 12:10; Hebr 6:4–6

[65] Wendelborn, Joachim von Fiore, pp. 92f.

[66] Wendelborn, Joachim von Fiore, pp. 29f.: Quasi–Chiliasmus

[67] Grundmann, Studien, p. 149

[68] Grundmann, Studien, pp. 112 & 114; Wendelborn, Joachim von Fiore, pp. 21f.

[69] Grundmann, Studien, p. 114

[70] Grundmann, Studien, pp. 414f.

[71] Joh 13:1f.

[72] Joh 6:54f.

[73] Grundmann, Studien, p. 112

[74] Wendelborn, Joachim von Fiore, p. 105f.

[75] Rev 7:2; cf. Ch. II, P. 1

[76] Wendelborn, Joachim von Fiore, p. 160

[77] Wendelborn, Joachim von Fiore, p. 160

[78] Wendelborn, Joachim von Fiore, p. 161

[79] Wendelborn, Joachim von Fiore, p. 161

[80] Cf. Wendelborn, Joachim von Fiore, pp. 161f.

[81] Grundmann, Herbert. *Ketzergeschichte des Mittelalters* (Die Kirche in ihrer Geschichte von Dietrich Schmitt und Ernst Wolf, Band 2, Lieferung G 1. Teil), 3rd Edition. Göttingen: 1978 (Grundmann, Ketzergeschichte), p. 22.

[82] Grundmann, Ketzergeschichte, p. 20

[83] Grundmann, Ketzergeschichte, pp. 22f.

[84] Franzen, Kirchengeschichte, p. 203

[85] Grundmann, Ketzergeschichte, p. 28f.

[86] Nigg, Walter. *Das Ewige Reich.* Erlenbach-Zürich:1944 (Nigg, Das Ewige Reich), pp. 173f.

[87] Nigg, Das ewige Reich, p. 174

[88] Nigg, Das ewige Reich, pp. 175f.

[89] Lützeler, Heinrich. *Die symbolische Franziskuslegende*. Munich/Berlin: 1929 (Lützeler, Franziskuslegende), p. 61f.

[90] Rev 7:2

[91] Lützeler, Franziskuslegende, p. 108

[92] Hildegard von Bingen. *Wisse die Wege*, 6th Edition. Salzburg: 1975, pp. 330f. incl. notes; Hildegard von Bingen. *Welt und Mensch*. Salzburg: 1965, pp. 300f.

[93] Huber, Harald. *Das Nardenöl aus dem Alabastergefäß. Von Tod und Auferstehung Christi ergriffen wie Maria*. Gelnhausen: 2007 (Huber, Nardenöl), pp. 76f.

[94] Franzen, August. *Kleine Kirchengeschichte* (Herderbücherei 237), 7th Edition. Freiburg i. Br.: 1978 (Franzen, Kirchengeschichte), p. 231

[96] Franzen, Kirchengeschichte, pp. 230f.

[97] Nigg, Das ewige Reich, pp. 345f.

[98] Nigg, Das ewige Reich, p. 348

[99] Nigg, Das ewige Reich, pp. 349f.

[100] Nigg, Das ewige Reich, p. 353

[101] Nigg, Das ewige Reich, p. 358

[102] Nigg, Das ewige Reich, p. 356

[103] Nigg, Das ewige Reich, p. 360

[104] Nigg, Das ewige Reich, p. 361

[105] Nigg, Das ewige Reich, p. 364

[106] Acts 1:9–11; Rev 1:7; 1Pet 3:22

[107] Rom 11:25; Lk 21:24

[108] Lk 21:25–28; Mt 24:3–31; esp. 24:29–31; Mk 13:24–27; (Isa 13:10; 34:4; Joel 2:10; Hag 2:6.21; 2Pet 3:10; Dan 7:13; Mt 26:64; Mk 14:62; Rev 1:7)

[109] Rom 11:25–32

[110] 1Cor 15:23–24

[111] 1Cor 15:51–58

[112] 1Cor 15:35–50

[113] Rom 8:18f.

[114] Nigg, Das ewige Reich, p. 183

[115] According to Hesemann, Michael. *Jesus von Nazareth*. Augsburg: 2009, p.74: 5 B.C. In an edition of the German "Einheitsübersetzung" translation of the Bible, under "VIII Zeittafel zur Geschichte des alten und neuen Bundes," the date 7/6 B.C. is given as the date for Christ's birth.

[116] Nigg, Walter. *Das mystische Dreigestirn: Eckhart, Tauler, Suso*. Zurich/Munich: 1988 (Nigg, Das mystische Dreigestirn), pp. 71f.

[117] Nigg, Das mystische Dreigestirn, p. 72

[118] Cf. Eckhart, Meister: *Deutsche Predigten und Traktate* (Josef Quint), 7th Edition. Hamburg: 2007 (Eckhart, Deutsche Predigten), p. 454 par. I; as well as Nigg, *Das mystische Dreigestirn*, pp. 75f.

[119] Störmer-Caysa, Uta. *Einführung in die mittelalterliche Mystik*. Stuttgart: 2004 (Störmer-Caysa, Mittelalterliche Mystik), pp. 123f.

[120] Eckehart, Deutsche Predigten, p. 256; Gnädinger, Louise. *Deutsche Mystik*. Zürich: 1989 (Gnädinger, Deutsche Mystik), pp. 159f.

[121] Cf. Huber, Das Nardenöl, pp. 71f., as well as the following rosary texts:

> "Hail, Mary, full of grace, the Lord is with thee: blessed art thou among women, and blessed is the fruit of thy womb,
>
> Jesus, whom you, O virgin,
>
> > conceived by the Holy Spirit and carried to Elizabeth
> >
> > gave birth to
> >
> > sacrificed in the temple
> >
> > found in the temple again.
>
> Jesus, who for us

sweated blood

was flogged

carried the heavy cross

was crucified.

Jesus, who

rose from the dead

ascended to heaven

sent us the Holy Spirit

(has all power)

(will return in glory)."

The sentences in parenthesis are today replaced by Marian texts.

The introductory text is no longer in line with modern Bible translations such as the New American Bible (Lk 1:28b and 1,42b): "Hail, favored one! The Lord is with you. Most blessed are you among women, and blessed is the fruit of your womb." As Eckhart emphasizes, Mary is not actually addressed by her name.

[122] Gal 2:20

[123] (Augustine, The City of God), XX 7. Augustinus, Aurelius / Augustine of Hippo. *The City of God / De Civitate Dei*, translated by Marcus Dods. New York: The Modern Library, a division of Random House, Inc., 1950

[124] Cf. Silesius, Angelus. *Gesammelte Werke,* 3rd Edition. Wiesbaden: 2002.

[125] Tauler, Johannes. *Predigten* (ed. by Georg Hofmann), 5th Edition. Einsiedeln: 2011, pp. 65f.

[126] Gnädinger, Deutsche Mystik, pp. 67f.

[127] Nigg, Dreigestirn, pp. 91f.

[128] E.g. Seuse, Heinrich. *Deutsche mystische Schriften.* Düsseldorf: 1986.

[129] Nigg, Dreigestirn, p. 151

[130] Nigg, Dreigestirn, p. 152

[131] Nigg, Dreigestirn, pp. 153f.

[132] This was a common abbreviation for Jesus at the time, influenced by the Greek. Cf. “IHS” in *Lexikon für Theologie und Kirche*, 2nd Edition. Freiburg i.Br.: 1964 (LThK).

[133] Nigg, Dreigestirn, p. 155

[134] Nigg, Dreigestirn, p. 157

[135] Nigg, Dreigestirn, p. 158

[136] Nigg, Dreigestirn, p. 160

[137] Nigg, Dreigestirn, p. 161

[138] Nigg, Dreigestirn, p. 162

[139] Nigg, Dreigestirn, p. 163

[140] Cf. Nigg, Dreigestirn, pp. 64f. & p. 176.

[141] Luther, Martin. *On the Freedom of a Christian*, translated by Henry Wace. In the public domain (Luther, Freedom); cf. Wehr, Gerhard. *Martin Luther, der Mystiker.* Munich: 1999, pp. 117f.

[142] Cf. Ch. I, B. c)

[143] Luther, Martin. *Martin Luther's Large & Small Catechism.* In the public domain (Luther, Catechism).

[144] Evangelische Reformierte Kirche: *Der Heidelberger Katechismus*, 5th Edition. Neukirchener Theology, Neukirchen-Vluyn: 2012 (Heidelberger Katechismus), pp. 21f. & 36f.

[145] Ch. VI, B. 4.

[146] Wallmann, Johannes. *Kirchengeschichte Deutschlands seit der Reformation*, 7th Edition. Tübingen: 2012 (Wallmann, Kirchengeschichte), p. 46.

[147] Wallmann, Kirchengeschichte, p. 47

[148] Cf. Augustine, City of God, XX 7; the end of Ch. IV.

[149] Wallmann, Kirchengeschichte, pp. 50f. & 77f.

[150] Wallmann, Kirchengeschichte, pp. 51f.

[151] Wallmann, Kirchengeschichte, pp. 77f.

[152] Dellsperger, Rudolf & Lavater, Hans Rudolf (ed.). *Die Wahrheit ist untödlich: Berner Täufer in Geschichte und Gegenwart*. Bern: Mennonitica Helvetica, 2007, pp. 122 & 125; cf. also pp. 138f. & pp. 152f.

[153] Cf. Wallmann, Johannes. *Der Pietismus*, 2nd Edition. Göttingen: 2005 (Wallmann, Pietismus).

[154] Wallmann, Pietismus, p. 21

[155] Wallmann, Pietismus, pp. 34 & 37

[156] Wallmann, Pietismus, p. 37

[157] Wallmann, Pietismus, p. 38

[158] Wallmann, Pietismus, p. 39

[159] Wallmann, Pietismus, p. 26

[160] Hegel, G.W.F.: *Werke 12, Vorlesungen über die Philosophie der Geschichte*. Frankfurt a.M.: 1970, pp. 386f.

[161] Ch. VIII

[162] Wallmann, Pietismus, p. 58

[163] Wallmann, Pietismus, pp. 60f.

[164] Wallmann, Pietismus, p. 62

165 Wallmann, Pietismus, p. 63

166 Wallmann, Pietismus, p. 64

167 Wallmann, Pietismus, pp. 64f.

168 Wallmann, Pietismus, p. 65

169 Wallmann, Pietismus, pp. 62f.

170 Wallmann, Pietismus, p. 67

171 Wallmann, Pietismus, p. 68

172 Wallmann, Pietismus, p. 77

173 Wallmann, Pietismus, p. 83

174 Wallmann, Pietismus, p. 84

175 Wallmann, Pietismus, p. 86

176 Wallmann, Pietismus, p. 97

177 Wallmann, Pietismus, p. 105

178 Wallmann, Pietismus, p. 108

179 Wallmann, Pietismus, p. 110

180 Wallmann, Pietismus, p. 114

181 Wallmann, Pietismus, p. 115

182 Wallmann, Pietismus, pp. 174f.

183 Wallmann, Pietismus, p. 177

184 Wallmann, Pietismus, p. 179

185 Wallmann, Pietismus, pp. 181f.

[186] Wallmann, Pietismus, p. 188

[187] Wallmann, Pietismus, p. 185

[188] Wallmann, Pietismus, p. 189

[189] Wallmann, Pietismus, p. 195; cf. also p. 200

[190] Wallmann, Pietismus, pp. 136f.

[191] Wallmann, Pietismus, p. 136

[192] Wallmann, Pietismus, pp. 141, 146f., 148f., 167

[193] Wallmann, Pietismus, p. 142

[194] Wallmann, Pietismus, p. 21

[195] Augustine, City of God, XX 7

[196] Denzinger, Heinrich & Hunermann, Peter. *A Compendium of Creeds, Definitions, and Declarations of the Catholic Church.* Ignatius Press, 2012, No.3839. The Roman Catechism interprets this as a prohibition—which, however, is not binding.

[197] Wallmann, Pietismus, p. 26

[198] Gal 2:20; Rom 8:9f.; Col 3:4

[199] Joh 14:6

[200] Beckmann-Zöller, Beate. *Pfingsten ist nicht vorbei. Sr. Elena Guerra – ihr Leben und ihr Briefwechsel mit Papst Leo XIII,* 1st Edition. Maihingen: CE Deutschland, 2009 (Beckmann-Zöller, Elena Guerra), pp. 6f.

[201] Beckmann-Zöller, Elena Guerra, pp. 15 & 18; cf. p. 4 of the chapter

[202] Beckmann-Zöller, Elena Guerra, pp. 20f.

[203] Beckmann-Zöller, Elena Guerra, p. 29

[204] Beckmann-Zöller, Elena Guerra, p. 48

[205] Beckmann-Zöller, Elena Guerra, p. 49

[206] Beckmann-Zöller, Elena Guerra, p. 50

[207] Beckmann-Zöller, Elena Guerra, pp. 107f.

[208] Beckmann-Zöller, Elena Guerra, p. 49

[209] Regarding the prayer for the Spirit, there is also Lk 11:13, besides Mt 7:7–11, which cannot be interpreted unambiguously.

[210] Brief papal letter to all bishops

[211] Beckmann-Zöller, Elena Guerra, p. 78

[212] Beckmann-Zöller, Elena Guerra, p. 79

[213] Translated from the Latin text.

[214] Beckmann-Zöller, Elena Guerra, p. 88

[215] Beckmann-Zöller, Elena Guerra, p. 53

[216] Beckmann-Zöller, Elena Guerra, p. 56

[217] Beckmann-Zöller, Elena Guerra, pp. 82f.

[218] "Come, Creator Spirit"

[219] Kollins, Kim. *Brennender Dornbusch, Die Rückkehr zum Obergemach in Anbetung und Fürbitte, Alzenau 2001* (Kollins, Dornbusch), p. 54 & p. 128 ('let sing').

[220] On 1.1.1901 there was a slightly different latin text. Furthermore cf. Cantalamessa, Raniero. *Komm, Schöpfergeist*, 2. ed. Freiburg, Basel, Wien 1999. (Canalamessa, Schöpfergeist).

[221] Cantalamessa, Schöpfergeist, p. 16

[222] Beckmann-Zöller, Elena Guerra, pp. 26f.

[223] Chasle, Louis. *Schwester Maria vom göttlichen Herzen Droste zu Vischering.* Aus dem Französischen übersetzt von P. Leo Sattler, Freiburg i.Br. 1907 (Chasle, Droste zu Vischering) p. 301. Pope Leo XIII. Encyclical *Annum sacrum* (Leo XIII, Annum sacrum).

[224] Pope Leo XIII. Encyclical *Mirae caritatis* (Leo XIII, Mirae caritatis).

[225] Leo XIII, Annum sacrum

[226] Pope Leo XIII. Encyclical *Divinum illud munus* (Leo XIII, Divinum illud munus).

[227] Cf. several chapters in Huber, Nardenöl; also Leo XIII, Annum sacrum; Pope Pius XII. Encyclical *Haurietis aquas* (Pius XII, Haurietis aquas).

[228] Huber, Nardenöl, pp. 131f.; Schwendimann, Friedrich. *Herz-Jesu-Verehrung heute?* Stein am Rhein: 1974 (Schwendimann, Herz-Jesu); Alacoque, Margareta Maria, *Leben und Offenbarungen von ihr selbst geschrieben und ergänzt durch Zeitgenossen,* Freiburg i.Ue. 1994 (Alacoque, Leben).

[229] Huber, Nardenöl, p. 133

[230] Huber, Nardenöl, p. 132; Alacoque, Leben, pp. 61f.

[231] Pius XII, Haurietis aquas

[232] Cf. esp. Pius XII, Haurietis aquas, par. 17, 19, 22, 23, 25, 26, 27.

[233] Chasle, Droste zu Vischering, p. 7; also p. 37

[234] Chasle, Droste zu Vischering, p. 8

[235] Lk 24:32

[236] Fiducia cum amico contracta

[237] Leo XIII, Annum sacrum, appendix; cf. also par. 7 of Annum sacrum

[238] Burgess, Dictionary, p. 356

[239] Burgess, Dictionary, pp. 354f., esp. 362

[240] Joh 13:23

[241] Joh 3:25

[242] Joh 6:22–59; esp. 32–34

[243] Joh 6:54–58

[244] Joh 6:63

[245] Lk 22:15f

[246] Joh 15:4f; Rom 8:9f; 1Cor 11:28; 2Cor 13:5; Gal 2:20; Col 3:4

[247] Ex 33:11; Deu 5:4 & 34:10; Gen 32:31: Jacob gives the name Penuel (face of God) to the place, saying, "Because I have seen God face to face, yet my life has been spared."

[248] Gal 2:20; Rom 8:9; Col 3:4

[249] Ch. XI, D. Faith Today

[250] Huber, Nardenöl, p. 13, notes 13, 14, 15 & p. 14

[251] Huber, Nardenöl

[252] Huber, Nardenöl, cf. esp. Ch. 2, 3, 11, 15, 16 & 17

[253] St. Gertrud von Helfta. *Gesandter der göttlichen Liebe*. Stein am Rhein: 1979 (Gertrud, Gesandter), pp. 322f.

[254] Pius XII, Haurietis aquas, par. 51

[255] Pius XII, Haurietis aquas, par. 53 & 54

[256] Huber, Nardenöl, pp. 135f; Schwendimann, Herz-Jesu, pp. 104f. & pp. 10–12

[257] See Ch. V, B. 2.

[258] Huber, Nardenöl, pp. 137f.; Kollins, Dornbusch, pp. 18–20; 53–55; 126–129; Synan, Vinson (ed.). *Aspects of Pentecostal-Charismatic Origins*, Plainfield, NJ: 1975, p. 195 (Synan, Aspects); Synan, Vinson: *The Holiness-Pentecostal Tradition*, 2nd Edition, Grand Rapids, Michigan: 1997, pp. 2–5; Hocken, Peter D. *Die Strategie des Heiligen Geistes?* Ravensburg 1998, pp. 111f; Zopfi, Jakob: ... *auf*

alles Fleisch: Geschichte und Auftrag der Pfingstbewegung, Kreuzlingen: 1985, pp. 25f.

[259] Synan, Aspects, p. 195

[260] Bartleman, Azusa Street.

[261] Bartleman, Azusa Street, p. 3

[262] Bartleman, Azusa Street, pp. 8 & 19

[263] Bartleman, Azusa Street, p. 16

[264] Cf. Ch. IV Pietism, A.

[265] Cf. Ch. VII, γ) Obedience; Col 1:24; Pope John Paul II. Apostolic Letter, On the Christian Meaning of Human Suffering (*Salvifici Doloris*).

[266] Mt 24:34: "This generation" probably refers to the people of Israel.

[267] Greek *apantesis*. Also in Mt 25:6 and Acts 28:15; cf. Ch. VII, par. B3.

[268] Mt 25:1f., cf. Acts 28:1f.

[269] Bartleman, Azusa Street, p. 8

[270] Bartleman, Azusa Street, p.15 & 31

[271] Cf. Ch. V. B. 2.

[272] Bartleman, Azusa Street, p. 23

[273] Bartleman, Azusa Street, p. 9

[274] Bartleman, Azusa Street, p. 14

[275] Bartleman, Azusa Street, pp. 27f

[276] Bartleman, Azusa Street, p. 50

[277] Bartleman, Azusa Street, p. 50

[278] Bartleman, Azusa Street, p. 6

[279] Bartleman, Azusa Street, p. 7

[280] Bartleman, Azusa Street, pp. 92f

[281] Bartleman, Azusa Street, p. 93

[282] Bartleman, Azusa Street, p. 101

[283] Bartleman, Azusa Street, p. 57

[284] Bartleman, Azusa Street, pp. 94f

[285] Bartleman, Azusa Street, pp. 96f

[286] Bartleman, Azusa Street, p. 95

[287] Bartleman, Azusa Street, p. 96

[288] Bartleman, Azusa Street, p. 97

[289] Mk 9:38–41; Lk 9:49f.

[290] Joh 21:15–23

[291] Gertrud, Gesandter, pp. 322f. (cf. Ch. V. C.)

[292] Acts 12:1f.

[293] Mk 3:17

[294] Joh 1:42

[295] Mt 17:1–9; Mk 9:2–10; Lk 9:28–36

[296] Rev 14:1–5

[297] Jam 5:7; Joel 2:23 & 31f.; Ch. I. B. b)

[298] Bartleman, Azusa Street, pp. 92f

[299] Rev 12:1

[300] Ch. I. E., notes 51 & 52

[301] Ch. I. B., note 8; note 9

[302] Reinecker, Fritz. *Lexikon zur Bibel*, 19th total edition, 2nd special edition. 1991 (Reinecker, Lexikon zur Bibel), p. 1126 / III.

[303] Synan, Vinson. *The Century of the Holy Spirit: 100 Years of Pentecostal and Charismatic Renewal, 1901–2001.* Nashville, Tennessee: 2001 (Synan, The Century), p. 2.

[304] Synan, Century, p. 3

[305] Synan, Century, p. 4

[306] Synan, Century, p. 17f.

[307] Ott, Dogmatik, pp. 357f; but cf. Ch. III. A.

[308] Ott, Dogmatik, pp. 387f.; Council of Trent, DH 1528 & 1530f.

[309] Joh 3:5; Tit 3:5f.; 2Cor 5:17; Gal 6:15; Eph 4:23f.; 1Cor 6:11; Joh 14:23; 15:5

[310] Cf. Huber, Nardenöl, esp. p. 14; Mt 26,19; Mk 14,9

[311] Jam 2,17: "So also faith of itself, if it does not have works, is dead."

[312] Cf. Bittlinger, Arnold. Papst und Pfingstler, Der römisch katholisch–pfingstliche Dialog und seine ökumenische Relevanz, Studien zur interkulturellen Geschichte des Christentums, Vol. 16. Frankfurt a.M./Bern/Las Vegas 1978 (Bittlinger, Papst und Pflingstler); the dialogue was supposed to be mostly about spirituality and the spiritual life (p. 26).

[313] Bittlinger, Papst und Pfingstler, p. 73

[314] Cf. Bittlinger, Papst und Pfingstler; There: Synon, pp. 73f.; Bouyer, p. 74; Mouléon, p. 75.

[315] Bittlinger, Papst und Pfingstler, p. 88

[316] Bittlinger, Papst und Pfingstler, p. 80

[317] Burgess, Dictionary, p. 655

[318] Burgess, Dictionary, p. 616

[319] Burgess, Dictionary, p. 614

[320] Gen 1f.

[321] Duffield, Guy P. & Van Cleave, Nathaniel M. *Grundlagen pfingstlicher Theologie*. Solingen 2003 (Duffield, Pfingstliche Theologie), pp. 57–64.

[322] Duffield, Pfingstliche Theologie, p. 57

[323] Duffield, Pfingstliche Theologie, p. 57

[324] Ex 1:1; Hebr 11:3; Neh 9:6; Col 1:15–17; Joh 1:3

[325] Duffield, Pfingstliche Theologie, p. 125

[326] Duffield, Pfingstliche Theologie, p. 126

[327] Cf. e.g. Behe, Michael J. *Darwin's Black Box: The Biochemical Challenge to Evolution*. Free Press, 2006; cf. also Kuhn, Wolfgang: *Stolpersteine des Darwinismus - Ende eines Jahrhundertirrtums*, 3rd Edition. Stein am Rhein: 1999.

[328] Stamps, Donald C. *Studienbibel.* Springfield, Missouri USA, 2013 (Stamps, Studienbibel),
p. 27.

[329] Stamps, Studienbibel pp. 28f

[330] Rahner, Karl & Vorgrimmler, Herbert. *Kleines Konzilskompendium*. Freiburg i.Br. 1966 (Rahner Karl, Konzilskompendium). Dogmatische Konstitution über die göttliche Offenbarung, Ch. 5, par. 18 (p. 377).

[331] Rahner Karl, Konzilskompendium. Dogmatische Konstitution über die göttliche Offenbarung, Ch. 2, par. 7 (p. 370).

[332] Burgess, Dictionary, pp. 936f.

[333] Burgess, Dictionary, p. 942

[334] Acts 2:38

[335] Burgess, Dictionary, p. 938

[336] See Ch. X. B. on the Tribulation, the Antichrist, and the wrath of God.

[337] Geneva Study Bible. German edition. Witten: SCM R. Brockhaus im SCM–Verlag, 2011. Commentary on 1Thess 4:12 about the second coming of Christ: "Though the view is widespread that Christians would be taken out of this world, after which Christ would return a third time for his 'second coming,' it is not, in fact, supported by Holy Scripture."

[338] Mt 25:6; Acts 28:15: In these verses, too, a Greek word for "air" is used that implies closeness (air) rather than distance (aether) to the earth.

[339] Acts 7:55f.

[340] Joh 8:51; 11:25f.

[341] Mt 24:29; Rev 6:12

[342] Acts 14:23; 13:2f; 2Cor 6:5; 11:27

[343] Mt 6:16–18

[344] Mt 3:13–17; Mk 1:9–11; Lk 3:2f & Mt 4:1–11; Lk 4:1–13

[345] Nigg, Walter. *Der verborgene Glanz*, 3rd Edition. Olten: 1974, pp. 84f.

[346] Mt 9:14; Mk 2:18–20; Lk 5:33–35

[347] Cf. on this topic: Buob, Hans. *Berufen zur Hingabe: Die evangelischen Räte*, 2nd Ed. Hochaltingen; Gyr, Meinrad. *Im Dienst der Liebe: Gedanken und Meditationen zu den evangelischen Räten*, 3rd Edition. Freiburg im Üechtland: 1987 (Gyr, ev. Räte). Both authors are priests in the Charismatic Renewal of the Catholic Church.

[348] Mt 5:3

[349] 2Cor 8:10

[350] 1Cor 7:29–31

[351] Lk 6:20

[352] Eph 5:3–5; Gyr, ev. Räte, p. 43

[353] Cf. Heid, Stefan. *Zölibat in der frühen Kirche: Die Anfänge einer Enthaltsamkeitspflicht für Kleriker in Ost und West*, 2nd Edition. Paderborn: 1998 (Heid, Zölibat).

[354] Heid, Zölibat, pp. 49–51; 80f.; 103f.; 128–130; 180–182; 255–258; 318–321; 1Cor 7:5 (abstinence in marriage)

[355] Gyr, ev. Räte, p. 43f.

[356] Gyr, ev. Räte, p. 41f.

[357] Gal 2:20; cf. Rom 8:9f.; Col 3:3f.

[358] Eph 6:5; Col 3:18–20; 3:22

[359] Hebr 13:17; Tit 2:5; 3:1; Rom 6:16; 1Pet 5:5

[360] Rom 13:1–7; Titus 3:1; 1Pet 2:13–17

[361] Joh 4:34

[362] Acts 7:55

[363] Mt 11:29f.

[364] Ps 23:2b & 5a

[365] Burgess, Dictionary, pp. 992f.; Synan, Century, pp. 357f.

[366] Burgess, Dictionary, pp. 358–60; Synan, Century, p. 687

[367] McConnell, D.R. *A Different Gospel*. Hendrickson Publishers, 1995, 6th ed. 2011 (McConnell, Different Gospel), pp. 6f

[368] McConnell, Different Gospel, p. 24

[369] McConnell, Different Gospel, p. 25

[370] Burgess, Dictionary, pp. 992f. – M.B. Eddy

[371] McConnell, Different Gospel, pp. 101f

[372] McConnell, Different Gospel, p. 104

[373] McConnell, Different Gospel, pp. 132f

[374] McConnell, Different Gospel, p. 139

[375] McConnell, Different Gospel, pp. 115f

[376] McConnell, Different Gospel, p. 149

[377] McConnell, Different Gospel, pp. 149f

[378] McConnell, Different Gospel, p. 156

[379] McConnell, Different Gospel, pp. 156f

[380] McConnell, Different Gospel, pp. 169f

[381] McConnell, Different Gospel, p. 174

[382] 2Cor 4:16–18

[383] 2Cor 12:2–6

[384] 2Cor 11:24–27

[385] Mt 10:38; 16:24; Mk 8:34; Lk 9:23

[386] Mt 16:25; Mk 8:35; Lk 9:24

[387] Acts 7:55f.

[388] Lk 24:32

[389] D.R.McConnell does not see this reference to God, nor its Pentecostal foundation, since he has a liberal Protestant background. Cf. his book A Different Gospel, pp. 180f. and 187.

[390] 1Joh 2:15–16; cf. the article 'Christ und Welt' in Stamps, Studienbibel, p. 2415

[391] 1Cor 3:10–15

[392] Rev 3:14f.

[393] Joh 4: 34; 6: 39

[394] Mt 16:24; Mk 8:34

[395] Acts 7:55

[396] 1Joh 2:18; 1Tim 4:1; 2Thess 2:3f

[397] Joh 10:25 – 30:37f; 5:36; 14:11–14

[398] Synan, Aspects: O'Connor, Edward, *The Hidden Roots of the Charismatic Renewal in the Catholic Churc*h, pp. 184f.

[399] Synan, Century, pp. 149f.

[400] Synan, Century, pp. 159f.

[401] Synan, Century, pp. 161f.

[402] See Ch. VII. A.

[403] Synan, Century, p. 164

[404] Synan, Century, p. 166

[405] Calvin, Johannes. *(Intitution christianae religionis) Unterricht in der christlichen Religion.* Übersetzt von Otto Weber, 6. Aufl. Neukirchen – Vluyn, 1997 (Calvin, Institutio), pp. III & 3 & 11; cf. Keller, Carl-A. *Calvin Mystique. Au coeur de la pensée du Réformateur*. Geneva 2001, (Keller, Calvin Mystique).

[406] Synan, Century, pp. 166f.

[407] Synan, Century, pp. 169f.

[408] Burgess, Dictionary, pp. 477–519

[409] Burgess, Dictionary, pp. 514f.

[410] Burgess, Dictionary pp. 515f.

[411] Burgess, Dictionary, p. 517

[412] Synan, Century: Dispensationalism is not mentioned in the index, nor is the term *rapture*. The reference to Scofield only mentions his remark that there had never been as many books about the Holy Spirit as during his own time. Premillennialism is mentioned once, but only in a cited text, without going into any detail.

[413] Huber, Willy & Fischer Karl: *Leben im Geist Seminar*, course booklet. Grünkraut: 2002.

[414] Sievers, Ernst. *Leben-im-Geist-Seminar*. Passau: Kommunikationsdienst.

[415] Hanusch, Helmut & Fischer Karl & Birkenhauer Martin. *Leben aus der Kraft des Heiligen Geistes*, course booklet, 1st Edition. Grünkraut: 2011.

[416] Cf. Wimber, John & Springer, Kevin (ed.). *Riding the Third Wave: What Comes after Renewal?* Marshall Pickering, 1987.

[417] Gallagher Mansfield, Patti. *As by a New Pentecost: The Dramatic Beginning of the*
Catholic Charismatic Renewal. Franciscan University Press, 1992 (Gallagher, Pentecost), pp.6f.

[418] Rahner, Karl & Vorgrimmler, Herbert. *Kleines Konzilskompendium*. Freiburg i.Br.: 1966 (Rahner Karl, Konzilskompendium), p. 137.

[419] Isa 11:2

[420] Slosser, Bob. *A Man Called Mr. Pentecost.* Bridge Publishing Inc. (Logos International) 1977 (Slosser, Mr. Pentecost), p. 2

[421] This was in 1947.

[422] Slosser, Mr. Pentecost, pp. 199f.

[423] Cf. Ch. V. A.

[424] Gallagher, Pentecost, p. 33

[425] Cf. Ranaghan, Kevin & Dorothy. *Catholic Pentecostals*. New York: 1969 (Ranaghan, Catholic Pentecostals), pp. 1f. & pp. 39f.

[426] Gallagher, Pentecost, pp. 9f.

[427] Gallagher, Pentecost, p. 35.

[428] Gallagher, Pentecost, p. 35

[429] Gallagher, Pentecost, p. 34.

[430] Sherrill, John L. *They Speak with Other Tongues*. Chosen Books, 2004 (Sherrill, Other Tongues).

[431] Gallagher, Pentecost, pp. 35f.

[432] Gallagher, Pentecost, p. 36.

[433] Gallagher, Pentecost, p. 37.

[434] Cf. Ch. IX. B.

[435] Cf. Ch. V. B. 2.

[436] Gallagher, Pentecost, pp. 35f.

[437] Gallagher, Pentecost; cf. Ch. V.

[438] Gallagher, Pentecost, pp. 37f.

[439] Cf. Ch. VII. B. 4. γ on the principle of obedience

[440] He calls it *"Abgeschiedenheit"* (solitude)

[441] Cf. Ch. VIII.

[442] Cf. Ch. II. C.

[443] Gallagher, Pentecost, p. 66.

[444] Gallagher, Pentecost, p. 42.

[445] Lk 1:46f., "My soul proclaims the greatness of the Lord; my spirit rejoices in God my savior. For he has looked upon his handmaid's lowliness; behold, from now on will all ages call me blessed. The Mighty One has done great things for me, and holy is his name. His mercy is from age to age to those who fear him, ..." etc.

[446] Gallagher, Pentecost, p. 35.

[447] Cf. Ch. II. C.

[448] Patti Gallagher refers to the following Bible passages: Mt 3:11; Mk 1:8; Lk 3:16; Joh 1:33; Acts 1:5 & 11:16, and finally 1Cor 12 – 14.

[449] Cf. Ch. IX. B.

[450] Gallagher, Pentecost, p. 36.

[451] Cf. Hathaway, David. *Prophetic Vision* (magazine). No. 67, Spring 2013. Dewsbury, UK.

[452] Stückelberger, Hansjörg. *Europas Aufstieg und Verrat: Eine christliche Deutung der Geschichte*. Aachen: 2011 (Stückelberger, Verrat), p. 325.

[453] Cf. Stückelberger, Verrat, p. 325.

[454] Mt 27:19

[455] Cf. Hesemann, Michael. *Das Fatima Geheimnis. Marienerscheinungen, der Papst und die Zukunft der Menschheit*, 4th Edition. Rottenburg: 2009 (Hesemann, Fatima). English translation: http://www.vatican.va/roman_curia/congregations/cfaith/documents/rc_con_cfaith_doc_20000626_message-fatima_en.html.

[455] Hesemann, Fatima, pp. 27f.

[456] Hesemann, Fatima, p. 45

[457] Hesemann, Fatima, p. 46

[458] Hesemann, Fatima, p. 74

[460] Hesemann, Fatima, pp. 75f.

[461] Hesemann, Fatima, p. 100

[462] Hesemann, Fatima, pp. 101f.

[463] Hesemann, Fatima, pp. 105f.

[464] Hesemann, Fatima, pp. 108f.

[465] Cf. Hesemann, Fatima, pp. 113f.

[466] Hesemann, Fatima, pp. 118f.

[467] Hesemann, Fatima, pp. 120f.

[468] Hesemann, Fatima, pp. 129f.

[469] Hesemann, Fatima, p. 134

[470] Hesemann, Fatima, p. 144

[471] Hesemann, Fatima, p. 153

[472] Hesemann, Fatima, pp. 158f.

[473] Hesemann, Fatima, p. 162f

[474] Hesemann, Fatima, p. 167

[475] Hesemann, Fatima, pp. 168f.

[476] Hesemann, Fatima, pp. 175f.

[477] Hesemann, Fatima pp. 181f.

[478] I only saw an angel twice in my life.

[479] Cf. Hathaway, Prophetic Vision, No.73, Fall 2014.

[480] Cf. Ch. D., note 466.

[481] Cf. Führer, Christian. *Und wir sind dabei gewesen: Die Revolution, die aus der Kirche kam*, 6th Edition. Berlin: 2014 (Führer, Revolution), esp. pp. 119f. & 174f. *frech, fromm, frei. Worte, die Geschichte schrieben*. Leipzig, 2013, pp. 23f. & 74f. *JoelNews* (magazine), 2014, No. 37, 38, 39.

[482] Joh 21:18

[483] Cf. "Kath. Kirche, Papstwahl," *Charisma* No. 164, bonus to p. 51.

[484] Cf. *CE-Info der Charismatischen Erneuerung in der katholischen Kirche* (magazine), I/2013, pp. 6 & 11 (report by Bruce Yocum, Goodnews No. 22, Nov 2012 – translated).

[485] Hathaway, Prophetic Vision, No. 68, Summer 2013.

[486] What he might have in mind is the "prophecy of Malachy," which probably goes back to Philipp Neri. Cf. Troll, Hildebrand. *Die Papstweissagung des Heiligen Malachias*, 4th Edition. Stein am Rhein: 1982 (Troll, Papstweissagung), pp. 94f.; the conclusion that this refers to a last pope was added much later by another person, cf. Ernst, Robert. *Die Papstweissagung des hl. Bischofs Malachias*, Markus-Verlag, 1955, pp. 93f. Then there is also a prediction by the astrologer Nostradamus, which I do not want to go into.

[487] JoelNews, No. 41, Dec 6, 2013

[488] Hesemann, Fatima, pp. 219f.

[489] Hesemann, Fatima, pp. 164f.

[490] Cf. Mk 13:24–27; Lk 21:25–28

[491] Ritter, Adolf Martin. *Kirchen und Theologiegeschichte in Quellen, Volume 1*. Alte Kirche, Neukirchen-Vluyn: 1977, pp. 30f; English translation based on Durdin-Robertson, Lawrence. *Communion with the Goddess: Initiation and the Mysteries*. Cesara Publications, 1976.

[492] Bochenski, J.M. *Contemporary European Philosophy*. University of California Press, 1969 (Bochenski, Philosophy).

[493] Bochenski, Philosophy, Ch. VI. 17. E. p. 167

[494] Bochenski, Philosophy, Ch. VI. 17. E. p. 168

[495] Bochenski, Philosophy, Ch. VI. 18. pp. 173f.

[496] Bochenski, Philosophy, Ch. VI. 18. G. p. 181

[497] Bochenski, Philosophy, Ch. I. 1. A. pp. 1f.

[498] "There is only one really serious philosophical question, and that is suicide."

[499] "Judging whether life is or is not worth living amounts to answering the fundamental question of philosophy."

[500] "This divorce between man and his life, the actor and his setting, is properly the feeling of absurdity."

[501] Drewermann, Eugen. *Ich steige hinab in die Barke der Sonne: Alt-ägyptische Meditationen zu Tod und Auferstehung in Bezug auf Joh 20-21*, 2nd Edition. Olten: 1989, pp. 90f.

[502] Castaneda, Carlos. *A Separate Reality*, Penguin Arkana 1990 (Castaneda, Reality), Ch. 10, pp. 157f & Ch. 13, pp. 201f.

[503] Castaneda, Reality, pp. 157f.

[504] Castaneda, Reality, pp.201f. (Mescalito is the spirit of the intoxicant marihuana.)

[505] Castaneda, Reality, pp. 202f.

[506] Castaneda, Reality, p. 204

[507] So 1:12; 4:13; cf. Huber, Nardenöl, pp. 13f.

[508] Ez 34:15

[509] Her real name was Helena Kowalska.

[510] Kowalska, Saint Maria Faustina. *Divine Mercy in My Soul: Diary of Sister M. Faustina Kowalska.* Marian Press, 2015 (Kowalska, Diary). Online version: https://www.faustyna.pl/zmbm/en/diary-full-text.

[511] Unfortunately, a popular image today portrays the Lord looking directly at the viewer with a lively posture, as was common in Baroque art. Cf. the German edition of Faustina's diary (Hauteville, 2000), page 4, note 1, and the images contained in the book; the cover shows the original.

[512] Faustina, Diary, pp. 139 par. 299

[513] Also of the Father. The "wrath of the Father" is not to be taken literally. What is meant is his justice. Not to mention that it was the Father who commanded the Son to be crucified for us! Perhaps it is also a reference to the "wrath of God" in Revelation.

[514] Cf. Joh19:34

[515] Faustina, Diary, p. 24 par. 50

[516] Faustina, Diary p. 121 par. 242

[517] Faustina, Diary, p. 24 par. 50, confer also p. 98 par. 177

[518] But: in answer to Mary's prayer, the time of grace is prolonged. See Faustina, Diary, p. 455 par. 1261.

[519] Faustina, Diary; abiding by the instruction of her father confessor, she always write the words of the Lord in italics.

[520] Faustina, Diary, p. 291 par. 723

[521] Faustina, Diary, p. 539 par. 1507

[522] Faustina, Diary, p. 455 par. 1264

[523] Faustina, Diary, p. 147 par. 324

[524] Faustina, Diary, p. 210 par. 482

[525] Faustina, Diary, p. 207 par. 476

[526] Faustina, Diary, p. 332 par. 848

[527] Faustina, Diary, p. 134 par. 281

[528] However, this does not apply to plans she made herself; cf. Faustina, Diary p. 228 par. 536.

[529] Faustina, Diary, p. 193 par. 437, endnote 96

[530] Faustina, Diary, p. 193 par. 438

[531] Faustina, Diary, p. 207 par. 476

[532] Faustina, Diary, p. 225 par. 526

[533] Faustina, Diary, p. 380 par. 991

[534] Faustina, Diary, p. 438 par. 1218

[535] *JoelNews*. No. 09, March 21, 2014 & No. 10, March 28, 2014.

[536] <https//www.youtube.com/watch?v=dHXKTKYunYo>

[537] <https//www.youtube.com/watch?v=NHbEWw7l_Ek>

[538] *L'Osservatore Romano* (German edition), August 29, 2014/No. 35; cf. "Historisches Ereignis, Papst bittet Pfingstgemeinden um Vergebung," *Idea*, 7/28/2014. www.idea.de/nachrichten/detail/thema-des-tages/artikel/ papst-trifft-evangelischen-pfarrer-in-caserta-82815.html. See bibliography: *Idea*, 7/28/2014, <www.erneuerung.de/index.php/116–ce–deutschland/oekumene/502–historisches–ereignis–papst– bittet–pfingstgemeinden–um–vergebung>.

[539] Düsseldorf 1999.

[540] Cf. Ch. VII. A.

Bibliography

Alacoque, Margareta Maria. *Leben und Offenbarungen von ihr selbst geschrieben und ergänzt durch Zeitgenossen*, Freiburg i.Ue. 1994 (Alacoque, Leben). (Alacoque, Margaret Mary. *The Autobiography of Saint Margaret Mary*. TAN Books & Publishers, 1995.)

Augustinus, Aurelius / Augustine of Hippo. *The City of God / De Civitate Dei*, translated by Marcus Dods. New York: The Modern Library, a division of Random House, Inc., 1950 (Augustine, The City of God).

Barrett, David B. & Kurian, George T. & Johnson, Todd M. *World Christian Encyclopedia*, 2nd Edition. Oxford: 2001 (Barrett, Encyclopedia).

Bartleman, Frank. *Azusa Street: How Pentecost Came to Los Angeles*. Bridge-Logos 1980 – EasyRead Large 16 (Bartleman, Azusa Street).

Baumert, Norbert & Bially Gerhard. *Pfingstler und Katholiken im Dialog. Die vier Abschlussberichte einer internationalen Kommission aus 25 Jahren.* Düsseldorf: 1999.

Beckmann-Zöller, Beate. *Pfingsten ist nicht vorbei. Sr. Elena Guerra – ihr Leben und ihr Briefwechsel mit Papst Leo XIII,* 1st Edition. Maihingen: CE Deutschland, 2009 (Beckmann-Zöller, Elena Guerra).

Behe, Michael J. *Darwin's Black Box: The Biochemical Challenge to Evolution.* Free Press, 2006.

Bittlinger, Arnold. "Papst und Pfingstler, Der römisch katholisch-pfingstliche Dialog und seine ökumenische Relevanz," *Studien zur interkulturellen Geschichte des Christentums*, Vol. 16. Frankfurt a.M./Bern/Las Vegas: 1978 (Bittlinger, "Papst und Pflingstler").

Bochenski, J.M. *Contemporary European Philosophy*. University of California Press, 1969 (Bochenski, Philosophy).

Buob, Hans. *Berufen zur Hingabe: Die evangelischen Räte*, 2nd Edition. Hochaltingen.

Burgess, Stanley M. & Van der Maas, Eduard M. *The New International Dictionary of Pentecostal and Charismatic Movements*, 2nd. Edition. Grand Rapids, Michigan: 2003 (Burgess, Dictionary).

Calvin, John. *Institutes of the Christian Religion / Institutio christianae religionis*, translated by John Allen. Philadelphia: Presbyterian Board of Publication, 1813 (Calvin, Institutio).

Cantalamessa, Raniero. *Komm, Schöpfergeist*, 2. ed. Freiburg, Basel, Wien 1999. (Canalamessa, Schöpfergeist).
(Cantalamessa, Raniero. *Come, Creator Spirit: Meditations on the Veni Creator*.
Liturgical Press, 2003).

Castaneda, Carlos. *A Separate Reality*, Reissue Edition. Washington Square Press, 1991 (Castaneda, Reality).

Chasle, Louis. *Schwester Maria vom göttlichen Herzen Droste zu Vischering.* Aus dem Französischen übersetzt von P. Leo Sattler, Freiburg i.Br. 1907 (Chasle, Droste zu Vischering).
(Chasle, Louis. *Sister Mary of the Divine Heart: Droste zu Vischering, Religious of the Good Shepherd, 1863–1899*. Benziger, 1906.)

Carter, Henry C. B. E. *Das Erbe Johannes Wesleys und die Oekumene*. Zürich, 1951 (Carter, Wesley).

CE-Info der Charismatischen Erneuerung in der katholischen Kirche (magazine), 1/2013.

Dellsperger, Rudolf & Lavater, Hans Rudolf (ed.). *Die Wahrheit ist untödlich, Berner Täufer in Geschichte und Gegenwart*. Bern: Mennonitica Helvetica, 2007.

Denzinger, Heinrich & Hunermann, Peter. *A Compendium of Creeds, Definitions, and Declarations of the Catholic Church.* Ignatius Press, 2012.

Duffield, Guy P. & Van Cleave, Nathaniel M. *Grundlagen pfingstlicher Theologie*. Solingen 2003 (Duffield, Pfingstliche Theologie). (Duffield, Guy P. & Van Cleave, Nathaniel M. *Foundations of Pentecostal Theology*. Creation House, 2008.)

Drewermann, Eugen. *Ich steige hinab in die Barke der Sonne: Alt-ägyptische Meditationen zu Tod und Auferstehung in Bezug auf Joh 20-21*, 2nd Edition. Olten: 1989.

Eckhart, Meister. *Deutsche Predigten und Traktate* (Josef Quint), 7th Edition. Hamburg: 2007 (Eckhart, Deutsche Predigten).

Ephraim, Bruder. *Nachsommerregen. Der Löwe von Juda: Die Geburt einer neuen Gemeinschaft*. Münsterschwarzbach: 1987 (Ephraim, Nachsommerregen).

Ernst, Robert. *Die Papstweissagung des hl. Bischofs Malachias*, Markus-Verlag, 1955.

Evangelische Reformierte Kirche: *Der Heidelberger Katechismus*, 5th Edition. Neukirchener Theology, Neukirchen-Vluyn: 2012 (Heidelberger Katechismus).

Franzen, August. *Kleine Kirchengeschichte* (Herderbücherei 237), 7th Edition. Freiburg i. Br.: 1978 (Franzen, Kirchengeschichte).

Friedell, Egon. *Kulturgeschichte Ägyptens und des Alten Orients*, 3rd Edition. Munich: 1980 (Friedell, *Kulturgeschichte Ägyptens*).

Führer, Christian. *Und wir sind dabei gewesen: Die Revolution, die aus der Kirche kam*, 6th Edition. Berlin: 2014 (Führer, Revolution).

Führer, Christian. *frech, fromm, frei: Worte, die Geschichte schrieben*. Leipzig: 2013.

Gallagher Mansfield, Patti. *As by a New Pentecost: The Dramatic Beginning of the Catholic Charismatic Renewal*. Franciscan University Press, 1992 (Gallagher, Pentecost).

Geneva Study Bible. German edition. Witten: SCM R. Brockhaus im SCM–Verlag, 2011.

Gnädinger, Louise. *Deutsche Mystik*. Zürich: 1989 (Gnädinger, Deutsche Mystik).

Grundmann, Herbert. *Ausgewählte Aufsätze Teil 2 Joachim von Fiore* (Schriften der Monumenta Germaniae Historica, Band 25, 2). Stuttgart: 1977 (Grundmann, Joachim von Fiore).

Grundmann, Herbert. *Ketzergeschichte des Mittelalters* (Die Kirche in ihrer Geschichte von Dietrich Schmitt und Ernst Wolf, Band 2, Lieferung G 1. Teil), 3rd Edition. Göttingen: 1978 (Grundmann, Ketzergeschichte).

Grundmann, Herbert. *Religiöse Bewegungen im Mittelalter*, 2nd Edition. Darmstadt: 1961 (Grundmann, Religiöse Bewegungen).

Grundmann, Herbert. *Studien über Joachim von Floris* (Beiträge zur Kulturgeschichte des Mittelalters und der Renaissance herausgegeben von Walter Goetz, Band 32). Leipzig/Berlin: 1927 (Grundmann, Studien).

Gyr, Meinrad. *Im Dienst der Liebe: Gedanken und Meditationen zu den evangelischen Räten*, 3rd Edition. Freiburg im Üechtland: 1987 (Gyr, ev. Räte).

Hathaway, David. *Prophetic Vision* (magazine). Dewsbury, UK.

Hegel, G.W.F. *Werke 12, Vorlesungen über die Philosophie der Geschichte*. Frankfurt a.M. 1970 (Hegel, Geschichte).

Heid, Stefan. *Zölibat in der frühen Kirche: Die Anfänge einer Enthaltsamkeitspflicht für Kleriker in Ost und West*, 2nd Edition. Paderborn: 1998 (Heid, Zölibat).

Litany of the Sacred Heart, approbated by Pope Leo XIII, 1899. www.kathpedia.com/index.php?title=Herz-Jesu-Litanei (Litany of the Sacred Heart).

Hesemann, Michael. *Das Fatima Geheimnis. Marienerscheinungen, der Papst und die Zukunft der Menschheit*, 4th Edition. Rottenburg: 2009 (Hesemann, Fatima).

Hildegard von Bingen. *Wisse die Wege*, 6th Edition. Salzburg: 1975.

Hildegard von Bingen. *Welt und Mensch*. Salzburg: 1965.

St. Gertrud von Helfta. *Gesandter der göttlichen Liebe*. Stein am Rhein: 1979 (Gertrud, Gesandter).

Höcht, Johannes Maria. *Die Große Botschaft von La Salette*, 4th Edition. Stein am Rhein: 1977/1996 (Höcht, *La Salette*).

Hocken, Peter D. *Brazing the Trail: Where is the Holy Spirit Leading the Church?* Bible Alive, 2001 (Hocken, Trail).

Huber, Harald. *Das Nardenöl aus dem Alabastergefäß: Von Tod und Auferstehung Christi ergriffen wie Maria*. Gelnhausen: 2007 (Huber, Nardenöl).

"Historisches Ereignis, Papst bittet Pfingstgemeinden um Vergebung," *Idea*, 7/28/2014. www.idea.de/nachrichten/detail/thema-des-tages/artikel/ papst-trifft-evangelischen-pfarrer-in-caserta-82815.html.

Jedin, Hubert. *Kleine Konzilsgeschichte*, Herder-Bücherei Band 51, 7th Edition. Freiburg/Basel/Vienna: 1966.

Joachim von Fiore. *Das Reich des Heiligen Geistes. Einführung von Alfons Rosenberg*. Bietigheim: 1977 (Joachim von Fiore, Das Reich).

"Kath. Kirche, Papstwahl," *Charisma* No. 164, bonus to p. 51.

"Historisches Ereignis: Papst bittet Pfingstgemeinden um Vergebung," *Charismatische Erneuerung in der Katholischen Kirche*, 8/3/2014. www.erneuerung.de/index.php/116-ce-deutschland/oekumene/502-historisches-ereignis-papst-bittet-pfingstgemeinden-um-vergebung.

Marc van der Woude. *JoelNews* (magazine), No. 41, 12/6/2013; No. 37 11/7/2014; No. 38, 11/14/2014; No. 39, 11/21/2014 (JoelNews).

Kamlah, Dr. Wilhelm. *Apokalypse und Geschichtstheologie: Die mittelalterliche Auslegung der Apokalypse vor Joachim von Fiore*. Berlin: 1935 (Kamlah, Apokalypse).

Keller, Carl-A. *Calvin Mystique, Au coeur de la pensée du Réformateur*. Geneva: 2001 (Keller, Calvin Mystique).

Kollins, Kim. *Brennender Dornbusch, Die Rückkehr zum Obergemach in Anbetung und*

Fürbitte, Alzenau 2001 (Kollins, Dornbusch).
(Kollins, Kim. *Burning Bush*. Humanomics, 2006.)

Kowalska, Saint Maria Faustina. *Divine Mercy in My Soul: Diary of Sister M. Faustina Kowalska.* Marian Press, 2015 (Kowalska, Diary).

Kuhn, Wolfgang. *Lexikon für Theologie und Kirche*, 2nd Edition. Freiburg i.Br.: 1964 (LThK).

Luther, Martin. *Martin Luther's Large & Small Catechism*. In the public domain (Luther, Catechism).

Luther, Martin. *On the Freedom of a Christian*, translated by Henry Wace. In the public domain (Luther, Freedom).

Lützeler, Heinrich. *Die symbolische Franziskuslegende*. Munich/Berlin: 1929 (Lützeler, Franziskuslegende).

McConnell, D.R. *A Different Gospel*. Hendrickson Publishers, 1994 (McConnell, Different Gospel).

MacCulloch, Diarmaid. *The Reformation*. Penguin Books, 2005 (McCulloch, Reformation).

Nigg Walter. *Das Ewige Reich*. Erlenbach-Zürich: 1944 (Nigg, Das Ewige Reich).

Nigg, Walter. *Das mystische Dreigestirn: Eckhart, Tauler, Suso*. Zurich/Munich, 1988 (Nigg, Das mystische Dreigestirn).

Nigg, Walter. *Der verborgene Glanz*, 3rd Edition. Olten: 1974.

O'Connor, Edward. *The Hidden Roots of the Charismatic Renewal in the Catholic Church.*

Ott, Ludwig. *Grundriss der Dogmatik*, 11. Ed., Bonn 2010 (Ott, Dogmatik).
(Ott, Ludwig. *Fundamentals of Catholic Dogma*. TAN Books, 1992)

Pope Leo XIII. Encyclical *Annum sacrum*. http://w2.vatican.va/content/leo-xiii/en/encyclicals/documents/hf_l-xiii_enc_25051899_annum-sacrum.html (Leo XIII, Annum sacrum).

Pope Leo XIII. Encyclical *Mirae caritatis*. http://w2.vatican.va/content/leo-xiii/en/encyclicals/documents/hf_l-xiii_enc_28051902_mirae-caritatis.html (Leo XIII, Mirae caritatis).

Pope Pius XII. Encyclical *Haurietis aquas*. http://w2.vatican.va/content/pius-xii/en/encyclicals/documents/hf_p-xii_enc_15051956_haurietis-aquas.html (Pius XII, Haurietis aquas).

Posener, Georges. *Lexikon der ägyptischen Kultur,* Wiesbaden 1960(?) (Posener, ägyptische Kultur).
(Posener, Georges. *Encyclopedia (Dictionary) of Egyptian Civilization.* Tudor Publishing Company, 1959.)

Prigent, Pierre. *Apocalypse 12, Histoire de l'exégèse*, in: *Beiträge zur Geschichte biblischer Exegese, Band 2*. Tübingen: 1959 (Prigent, Apocalypse 12).

Rahner, Hugo. *Symbole der Kirche: Die Ekklesiologie der Väter*. Salzburg: 1964 (Hugo Rahner, Ekklesiologie).

Rahner, Karl & Vorgrimmler, Herbert. *Kleines Konzilskompendium*. Freiburg i.Br.: 1966 (Karl Rahner, Konzilskompendium).

Ranaghan, Kevin & Dorothy. *Catholic Pentecostals*. NewYork: 1969 (Ranaghan, Catholic Pentecostals).

Reinecker, Fritz. *Lexikon zur Bibel*, 19th total edition, 2nd special edition. 1991 (Reinecker, Lexikon zur Bibel).

Ritter, Adolf Martin. *Kirchen und Theologiegeschichte in Quellen, Band 1*. Alte Kirche, Neukirchen-Vluyn: 1977.

Schwendimann, Friedrich. *Herz-Jesu-Verehrung heute?* Stein am Rhein: 1974.

Suso, Heinrich. *Deutsche mystische Schriften*. Düsseldorf: 1986 (Suso, Mystische Schriften).

Sherrill, John L. *They Speak with Other Tongues*. Chosen Books, 2004. (Sherrill, Other Tongues)

Sievers, Ernst. *Leben im Geist Seminar*. Kommunikationsdienst, Passau.

Silesius, Angelus. *Gesammelte Werke, 3rd Edition.* Wiesbaden: 2002 (Silesius Angelus, Werke).

Slosser, Bob. *A Man Called Mr. Pentecost.* Bridge Publishing Inc. (Logos International), 1977 (Slosser, Mr. Pentecost).

Stamps, Donald C. *Studienbibel.* Springfield, Missouri USA, 2013 (Stamps, Studienbibel).
(Stamps, Donald C. *Fire Bible: Global Study Edition.* Hendrickson Publishers, 2010.)

Störmer-Caysa, Uta. *Einführung in die mittelalterliche Mystik.* Stuttgart: 2004 (Störmer-Caysa, Mittelalterliche Mystik).

Stückelberger, Hansjörg. *Europas Aufstieg und Verrat: Eine christliche Deutung der Geschichte*. Aachen: 2011 (Stückelberger, Verra*t*).

Synan, Vinson. *The Century of the Holy Spirit: 100 Years of Pentecostal and Charismatic Renewal, 1901-2001*. Nashville, Tennessee: 2001 (Synan, Century).

Synan, Vinson (ed.). *Aspects of Pentecostal-Charismatic Origins*. Plainfield, NJ: 1975 (Synan, Aspects).

Troll, Hildebrand. *Die Papstweissagung des Heiligen Malachias*, 4th Edition. Stein am Rhein: 1982 (Troll, Papstweissagung).

Vatican City. *L'Osservatore Romano* (German edition), edited by: I-00120. Schwabenverlag, Ostfildern: 1971–present.

Wallmann, Johannes. *Kirchengeschichte Deutschlands seit der Reformation*, 7th Edition. Tübingen: 2012 (Wallmann, Kirchengeschichte).

Wallmann, Johannes. *Der Pietismus*, 2nd Edition. Göttingen: 2005 (Wallmann, Pietismus).

Wehr, Gerhard. *Martin Luther, der Mystiker*. Munich: 1999.

Wendelborn, Franz. *Gott und Geschichte: Joachim von Fiore und die Hoffnung der Christenheit*. Leipzig: 1974 (Wendelborn, Joachim von Fiore).

Wilkerson, David. *The Cross and the Switchblade*. Jove, 1986. (Wilkerson, Cross and Switchblade).

Wimber, John & Springer, Kevin (ed.). *Riding the Third Wave: What Comes after Renewal?* Marshall Pickering, 1987.

Zopfi, Jakob. ... *auf alles Fleisch: Geschichte und Auftrag der Pfingstbewegung.* Kreuzlingen: 1985.

For more information contact:

Harald Huber
C/O Advantage Books
P.O. Box 160847
Altamonte Springs, FL 32716

info@advbooks.com

To purchase additional copies of this book visit our bookstore website at: www.advbookstore.com

Longwood, Florida, USA
"we bring dreams to life"™
www.advbookstore.com

CPSIA information can be obtained
at www.ICGtesting.com
Printed in the USA
BVOW09s1810231017
498412BV00006B/446/P

9 781597 553940